GREEN

GREEN

A Field Guide
to Marijuana

Written by
Dan Michaels

Photography by
Erik Christiansen

ISBN 978-1-4521-3405-5

Manufactured in China.

Designed by Pentagram, New York

10 9 8 7 6 5 4

Chronicle Books LLC
680 Second Street
San Francisco, CA 94131

www.chroniclebooks.com

Introduction   p/6

PRIMER   p/9
Cannabis Overview

BUDS   p/49
Cannabis Strains

Resources   p/342

Introduction

Marijuana, pot, weed, bud, green—call it what you will, but the popularity of cannabis is at an all-time high. We have finally reached the tipping point where the negative myths and stereotypes are being debunked and the positive influences marijuana has on modern medicine, local economies, individual creativity, and our society as a whole can no longer be denied. And although marijuana still remains a source of controversy, there has never been a better time than right now to be a pot smoker.

One of the oldest, most recognized, and versatile plants on earth, cannabis is used for religious, medicinal, industrial, and recreational purposes. It has been cultivated, consumed, and enjoyed by mankind since the beginning of our recorded history. It has affected ancient cultures, languages, and continues to unite the human spirit by transcending gender, race, physical, social, and economic differences. From corporate magnates to blue-collar workers, country musicians to rap artists, hipsters to hippies, and everyone in between—marijuana is one of the few things we all share and enjoy together.

Today, we are in the midst of a "green" revolution where new strains of cannabis are being cultivated to produce desirable characteristics, unique traits, groundbreaking medicinal applications, and off-the-charts potency. And the quality and variety of strains available for the majestic flower of the female cannabis plant is astonishing. This dizzying array of hundreds, if not thousands of cannabis strains can be an experienced toker's dream or leave a novice user dazed and confused.

How do we navigate through this modern marijuana landscape? What are the differences between various cannabis strains? Should we care whether we smoke an indica versus a sativa? What makes all these new hybrid strains so special?

This field guide is here to help demystify this hazy cloud of uncertainty by outfitting you with the tools and knowledge necessary for selecting and enjoying the best buds. You don't need to be a cannabis grower, breeder, or "weedophile" to understand that characteristics such as appearance, smell, taste, and wide-ranging psychoactive effects all play an important role in the quality of the herb you choose. In order to truly appreciate cannabis, it is essential to understand the unique characteristics each different strain has to offer and how these characteristics are expressed when smoked or consumed.

Ultimately, it's feeling the positive psychoactive effects of cannabis that we all desire. These effects are both psychological and physiological—mind and body—and can range from relieving pain or stress, to feeling creative or euphoric, to being stoned or high. While these effects are often subjective, influenced by experiences and expectations, we can often anticipate or even predetermine what effects we should expect simply by educating ourselves on what strain we are about to smoke. This knowledge is vital to ensure that both recreational and medical marijuana users have the best experience possible.

Much like drinking alcohol, where the effects we feel vary drastically depending on how much we drink (quantity); who we are drinking with (experience); where we are drinking (surroundings); and what type(s) of alcohol we are drinking (expectation)—the same holds true for marijuana strains. Quantity, experience, surroundings, and expectations all play an important role in our overall enjoyment. But in the case of cannabis, quality holds the throne. The difference between smoking a dank sinsemilla or some dry schwag can mean the difference between feeling nice and lifted or feeling bugged out and paranoid.

Thankfully, we are no longer in a time in which we need to settle for any old weed. Cannabis is now in full bloom, a pot paradise where we can pick and choose exactly what we like and don't like—the pungent aroma of a **Skunk** strain, the spicy fragrance of a **Kush** strain, the sour taste of a **Diesel** strain, the smooth smoke of a **Haze** strain, the energized high of an heirloom **Sativa** strain, the stoned relaxation of a Landrace **Indica** strain, and everything in between. The choice is now in our own hands—to grind up, smoke, and enjoy.

We hope this field guide will not only provide some enlightenment about this sublime plant, but also act as a small step forward toward legitimizing what has become a source of contention among the misguided and miseducated.

It is high time to start exploring the wonderful world of weed.

PRIMER

Cannabis Overview

In order to truly appreciate and enjoy all the wonderful things marijuana has to offer, we must first lay a healthy foundation of knowledge on which to build our experiences. Lies, propaganda, and misinformation about marijuana have proliferated throughout history and it is only through proper education and the sharing of accurate information that we can start to undo the harm this has caused. Famous scientist and botanist George Washington Carver wisely said, "Education is the key to unlock the golden door of freedom." Hopefully, with the help of the enlightenment provided in this book, we can all continue to spread the truth that has already begun turning this key.

What Is Marijuana?

Figuratively, marijuana is earth's greatest gift to mankind. Physically, marijuana is a natural body and mind–altering treat. Literally, marijuana is the budding flower of the female cannabis plant.

But what makes marijuana so desirable is that it naturally produces a multitude of diverse chemical compounds called "phtyo-cannabinoids." When consumed, these cannabinoids produce a variety of wide-ranging effects on the human mind and body by activating and stimulating our body's internal cannabinoid receptors. All humans and animals naturally possess these "endo-cannabinoids" receptors. This complex cannabinoid system is the very reason cannabis has been consumed for both recreational and medicinal purposes by ancient cultures and modern societies alike.

The most well-known cannabinoid is called delta 9-tetrahydrocannabinol (THC). It is the psychoactive chemical that produces the desirable "high" or "stoned" feeling when consumed.

The other primary cannabinoid is known as cannabidiol (CBD). It has been found to be an effective treatment for a wide range of health conditions and thanks to modern scientific research, we've finally been able to quantify and prove these health benefits.

7,000 BC
First known use of cannabis plant in China.

0
Number of deaths caused from using marijuana.

75+
Number of diverse chemical compounds, called cannabinoids, found naturally in cannabis.

14%
Average THC potency found in marijuana compared to 1% in the 1970s.

1937

Year the U.S. federal government passed the Marijuana Tax Stamp Act making marijuana illegal.

1/3

The total worldwide cannabis cultivation and production that takes place in North America.

$300

Average price for an ounce of marijuana in the United States.

1996

Year California passed Prop 215, making it the first state ever to legalize marijuana for medicinal use.

1,000+

Estimated number of different marijuana strains created.

220m+

Estimated number of adult marijuana users worldwide according to the United Nations.

420

Cannabis culture's universally accepted time (4:20) to enjoy marijuana and date (April 20) to observe and celebrate cannabis.

2014

Year Colorado became the first state to sell legalized marijuana for recreational use.

Basic Plant Anatomy

The botany of the cannabis plant can be as mysterious and complex as, well, cannabis itself. Unless you're a botanist, the differences between a *stipule* and *calyx* may be too much information to really care about. That being said, to truly appreciate its natural wonder, all marijuana tokers should have some token of understanding about this amazing plant's structure. So here's the rundown of what is vital:

A. Flowers
The flowers, or buds, of the female cannabis plant is what we harvest, manicure, dry, cure, and ultimately consume. These buds hold the highest concentrations of cannabinoids with the most notable being THC. The largest bud that grows at the very top of the plant is called the "cola."

B. Trichomes and Pistils
All the chemical compounds found on the bud are encased within the tiny resin glands or "crystals" (called *glandular trichomes*) seen on the surface of the bud. The red or white "hairs" (called *pistils*) that grow out of the bud are a sign of a well-grown plant but do not contain any cannabinoids and are not an indicator of potency.
B1. *Trichomes*
B2. *Pistils*

C. Fan Leaves
The fan leaves are the big, beautiful, ubiquitous leaves we see everywhere being used as the unofficial logo for marijuana. Other than being a visual symbol for cannabis, the fan leaves' job is to "fan out" and take in all the light the plant needs to grow. Fan leaves do not contain any significant levels of THC so they won't give you any psychoactive effects and are typically discarded after harvesting.

D. Leaf Anatomy
The fan leaf has become the iconic and universal symbol for pro-marijuana. The individual leaves themselves are serrated and there are usually seven or nine leaflets per healthy fan leaf(there can be as many as eleven). Here's the basic structure of our beloved leaf:
D1. *Leaflets*
D2. *Bracts*
D3. *Petiole*

E. Sugar Leaves
Unlike the fan leaf, the small sugar leaf actually contains a good amount of cannabinoids because it grows within the bud itself and gets coated with trichomes, which gives it the appearance of being covered in sugar. Most of the sugar leaves are pruned away from the bud when harvested and are used to make edibles like cookies and brownies or concentrates like hash and wax.

F. Stems
Buds grow in clusters at the end of each stem. Stems support the buds structurally but also store important nutrients and help transport water from the roots. After all their hard work, the stems are often discarded since they contain little to no THC.

G. Seeds
The seeds produced by the cannabis plant are typically half male and half female. A female plant won't produce seeds if pollination from a male plant is prevented. Often referred to as sinsemilla, these seedless buds tend to grow larger with higher resin and cannabinoid content, making them more desirable. Besides being used to grow new plants, cannabis seeds are a nutritious food and a good source of protein. The oil made from cannabis seeds can also be used as a renewable fuel source.

H. Stalks
Much like the stem, the stalk is also useless for consumption. However, the long fibers found in the inner bark of the stalk, called hemp, can be utilized in other ways. Hemp is an extremely strong, durable, and versatile fiber that is used to make paper, rope, oil, biodegradable plastics, clothing, and other textiles.

What Are Strains?

A marijuana strain is simply a particular variety of the cannabis plant. Not so simple is the breeding process and genetic makeup within each strain. Lucky for us all there are master growers, creative breeders, and other amazing minds hard at work behind the scenes hunting for, cloning, and creating all the super strains that are available to all of us today.

But you don't need to be an expert to understand that all strains fall into one of three main categories: (1) **sativa**, (2) **indica**, or (3) **hybrid**. Sativa and indica strains are the two main naturally occurring species, and hybrid strains are a mix of the two. As new hybrid strains are developed they are crossbred with other existing strains, giving growers endless opportunities to experiment and produce the next great strain. No matter if a strain is a natural variety or a hybrid, each will have very specific qualities and unique psychoactive effects (*What's Your Phenotype,* see page 18).

As more and more strains become available, it can seem overwhelming to figure out which ones are best to procure and enjoy. You obviously can't rely on all the crazy and unusual names given to these strains, so what do you do? For starters, it's best to begin by narrowing down your choice to the variety type.

Sativas are known for being a "daytime" strain because they provide you with an uplifting and energetic head high. Indicas on the other hand are a better "nighttime" strain and will get your body stoned, making you feel relaxed, mellow, or even sleepy.

Hybrids provide a combination of effects that depend on the strains' lineage—their parents. Typically these hybrids are either indica or sativa dominant, meaning they will express the characteristics of the dominant variety with less characteristics of the secondary variety. An indica-dominant hybrid might give you a strong body buzz without feeling tired, or a sativa-dominant hybrid may make you very sociable and cheerful but still calm and relaxed. Other times, a hybrid can be a "true" hybrid, meaning that it is an even mix of both varieties.

CANNABIS IS CLASSIFIED INTO THREE SPECIES: SATIVA, INDICA, OR RUDERALIS.

The cannabis we love to smoke is either indica, sativa, or usually a hybrid of the two.

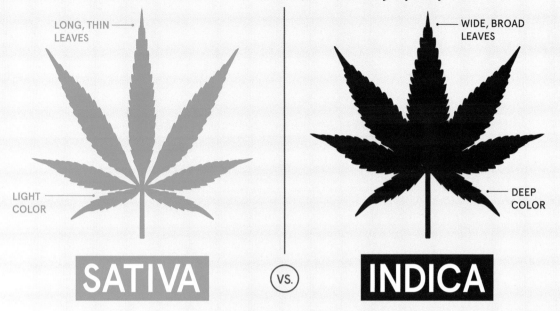

LONG, THIN LEAVES

LIGHT COLOR

SATIVA

WIDE, BROAD LEAVES

DEEP COLOR

INDICA

VS.

RUDERALIS *is a short, hearty, wild strain with fewer leaves and low THC content. It is not used for consuming but is sometimes crossbred with indicas or sativas to produce an "autoflowering" hybrid—meaning it will produce flowers (buds) based on age rather than light cycles like sativas or indicas.*

GROWING

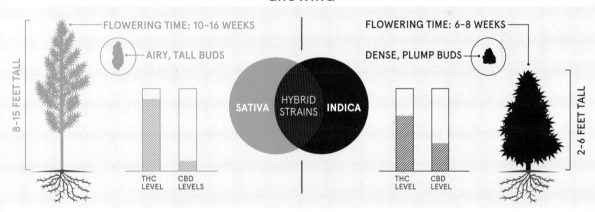

FLOWERING TIME: 10-16 WEEKS

AIRY, TALL BUDS

8-15 FEET TALL

THC LEVEL   CBD LEVELS

SATIVA   HYBRID STRAINS   INDICA

FLOWERING TIME: 6-8 WEEKS

DENSE, PLUMP BUDS

THC LEVEL   CBD LEVEL

2-6 FEET TALL

EFFECTS

DAYTIME: MIND/HIGH

CREATIVE
ALERT
ENERGETIC
EUPHORIA
SOCIABLE
CHEERFUL

COUCH-LOCK
SLEEPY
RELAXED
CAREFREE
CALM
MELLOW

NIGHTTIME: BODY/STONED

What's Your Phenotype?

The term *phenotype* or *"pheno"* will inevitably come up when talking about cannabis strains. It's one of those heady words that is actually pretty basic in concept but very complex in nature. By definition, a phenotype is simply any living thing's observable characteristics. In the cannabis plant these traits include size, shape, color, THC content, bud density, flavor, and smell to name a few. All these various traits can come together in a multitude of combinations adding to the complexity and variety of strains.

Seeing and smoking an assortment of strains will help you to start noticing these distinctions in phenotypes and more importantly help you to figure out what traits you like or don't like. If you prefer an energetic high, a pure sativa strain like **Durban Poison** (see **p/166**) will carry that trait. Or if you prefer the mellowing smoke of an indica strain, than maybe a strain like **Platinum OG** (see **p/298**) is worth trying. There are even strains bred with amazing flavors like **Bubble Gum** (see **p/114**) or **Blueberry** (see **p/104**).

It's the strain's unique combination of phenotypes that makes each strain so distinct and special. Each strain is carefully bred to express very specific trait combinations with all this information stored right into its own DNA. This unique genetic makeup—referred to as the strain's "genotype"—is what allows the same strain to be grown again and again. The genetics will always be the same but sometimes the phenotypes can vary—this is what you call "variations in phenotype."

Variation in phenos in the same strain is okay, but if they're completely different than either the plant was improperly grown or you're not getting what you paid for. This is why educated smokers talk about phenotypes and why it's so important to know which phenos to look for when trying new strain varieties.

For example, every bud shown here is the same strain called **Girl Scout Cookies** (see **p/182**). Each bud came from the same genetic code but is grown from different producers or crops. As you can clearly see, not all buds from the same genotype will look or behave the same. This is why when you buy Girl Scout Cookies from one source, that bud's characteristics may vary slightly from the same strain bought elsewhere. Maybe the color is slightly off, or perhaps the smell is more pungent, or maybe the effects don't last as long.

Why? Most often, it's the environment that directly affects a strain's phenotypes. Things like where the plant was grown, soil conditions, fertilizers, even the light or water source can directly effect the strain's inherent ability to properly express its desired traits—some may be suppressed while others may be exaggerated. Ultimately, it's how these phenotypes are revealed that will determine whether or not you have an award winning bud or a poorly grown dud.

INDOOR VS. OUTDOOR

Buds 1, 2, and 3 were grown indoors while buds 4, 5, and 6 were grown outdoors.

Plants grown indoors use artificial light under a completely closed environment—soil, water, fertilizers, even temperature and carbon dioxide levels are monitored and controlled. This method often produces strains coated in precise crystals with very high potency and consistent phenotypes throughout the crop.

Outdoor strains on the other hand use natural sunlight and interact with the terroir, the unique land and climate of a specific location. This produces larger plants that are generally more robust to combat Mother Nature's variables like wind and weather. The flavors and resin glands are also often more complex and viscous.

Simply put, indoor growing is more scientific while outdoor growing is more artisanal. Either way, if the cannabis plant is grown properly and to its full potential, the resulting buds will be spectacular.

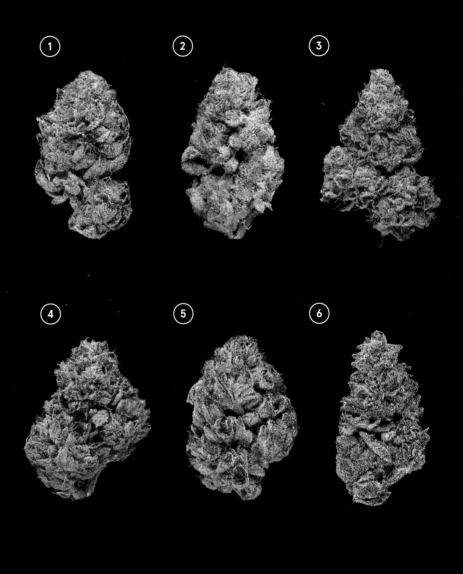

Beyond THC
The Entourage Effect

The cannabis plant's chemical compounds are what make it so magical, and these unique cannabinoids are found nowhere else in nature. While THC may be the most famous feel-good cannabinoid since 1964, isolated then by prized chemist Raphael Mechoulam, more recent research has isolated over 75 other unique cannabinoids from cannabis.

Klaas Hesselink and Derek Houston of Cannatest, based in Western Washington, provide cannabinoid analysis to determine cannabinoid profiles or fingerprints of cannabis strains. Klaas and Derek stress that nature put a TEAM of molecules in the cannabis plant that work together to create an effect that these molecules cannot effectively do alone. This team effort is called "The Entourage Effect" (coined by Dr. Mechoulam). A good example to illustrate this effect is the fact that a high 21% THC flower with 3% of cannabigerol (CBG), may actually feel less potent than a 16% THC flower with 1% cannabichromene (CBC) or fewer of the other modulating cannabinoids. Here's what else these experts have to say: Cannabis chemistry is like alcohol chemistry; we have established that each cannabinoid contributes to a different pharmacological effect, so it makes sense that mixing these chemicals at varying ratios will change the user's experience. For example, drinking a heavily hopped IPA beer will likely relax and tire one in the same way as a heavy CBG-filled Kush strain might. Or a high THC combined with high tetrahydrocannabivarin (THCV) may provide an energy-filled night similar to drinking tequila or a vodka energy drink, while high levels of CBC and THC may give more of a dreamy sensation, like an absinthe. Furthermore, as with alcohol, a person's own body chemistry will make an important difference in the overall experience.

POTENCY PERCENTAGES

The strength or potency of each cannabinoid is measured through a process called chromatography, which separates and measures each cannabinoids percent of weight compared to the overall weight of the sample. Percentages and ratios will vary with each strain but here are the typical breakdowns found in most buds:

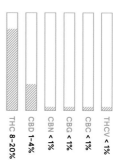

THC 8–20% CBD 1–4% CBN <1% CBG <1% CBC <1% THCV < 1%

Major Cannabinoids

THC
Delta 9-tetrahydrocannabinol

Therapeutic effects: analgesic (pain relief), neuroprotective, antioxidant, anti-inflammatory, appetite stimulant

It is the primary psychoactive component responsible for the "high" effect. It amplifies all sensory functions such as sight, hearing, color sensitivity, and increases arousal and a greater sense of well-being. This component produces strong feelings of euphoria, sharpens the mind, and promotes creativity.

CBD
Cannabidiol

Therapeutic effects: anti-convulsive, anti-spasmodic, antidepressant, anti-tumoral, sedative, neuroprotective

Not psychoactive, CBD works antagonistically in the micromolar range; it has an opposite effect of THC and provides no high to users. It actually reduces the psychoactive effect of THC, but in contrast, it prolongs the "high" effect. CBD is effective against anxiety and stress as well as causing strong muscle relaxation, especially in the smooth muscle fibers, therefore reducing muscle spasms. Concentrated CBD extract is also a highly effective anti-seizure treatment.

Minor Cannabinoids

CBN
Cannabinol

Therapeutic effects: analgesic, antibiotic, sedative, anti-convulsive, anti-inflammatory, antibacterial

It is mildly psychoactive and, just like aspirin (but three times as strong), CBN is a non-narcotic-type analgesic and is effective at relieving tension headaches. CBN is a breakdown product of THC. During storage (aging) CBN will slowly increase as THC deteriorates.

CBG
Cannabigerol

Therapeutic effects: sedative, analgesic, antibacterial, antifungal, anti-tumoral

CBG is the precursor form of a few of the other cannabinoids including THC and CBG, CBG tends to be higher in low THC "hemp" plant varieties and has thus far been found only in trace amounts in most marijuana strains.

CBC
Cannabichromene

Therapeutic effects: anti-inflammatory, analgesic, anti-depressant, sedative

CBC is a nonpsychoactive cannabinoid that also potentiates THC. It interacts in an as yet unknown way with THC to make the "high" more intense and pronounced. It is also considered a strong sedative and pain reliever.

THCV
Tetrahydrocannabivarin

Therapeutic effects: appetite suppressant, stimulant, anti-convulsive, anti-inflammatory

A psychoactive cannabinoid found along with THC in cannabis, research has shown that, in low doses, THCV will increase the effects of THC (strongly potentiating THC, provoking a heavy, stronger, and faster "high" effect). In larger doses, however, THCV is believed to oppose the effects of THC.

Terpenoids
Aromas, Flavors, and Therapeutic Effects

In addition to cannabinoids, the components of the cannabis plant's essential oils, called terpenoids, play an important therapeutic role in the overall entourage effect. The aromas and flavors of any given cannabis strain also depend on which terpenoids predominate. While nearly 20,000 terpenoid compounds have been found in all types of plant life, just over 200 of these terpenes have been identified in cannabis with the following eight occurring in significant amounts and most frequently.

Alpha-pinene
Also found in Pine needles
Flavors: piney, rosemary
Therapeutic effects: anti-inflammatory, antibacterial, aids memory, bronchodilator (aids breathing)

Beta-caryophyllene
Also found in echinacea
Flavors: citrus, oily, spicy
Therapeutic effects: anti-inflammatory, gastric cytoprotectant (cell protectant)

Caryophyllene Oxide
Also found in lemon balm
Flavors: clove, peppery, spicy, woody
Therapeutic effect: Antifungal

Limonene
Also found in lemons
Flavors: citrus, juniper, lemon, peppermint, rosemary, tangerine
Therapeutic effects: immune stimulant, antidepressant, antianxiety

Linalool
Also found in lavender
Flavors: candy spice, floral, herbal
Therapeutic effects: antianxiety, anticonvulsant, sedative

Myrcene
Also found in hops
Flavors: acrid, citrus, clove, fruity
Therapeutic effects: anti-inflammatory, sedative, analgesic (pain relief)

Nerolidol
Also found in oranges
Flavors: berry, floral, sweet, woody
Therapeutic effects: sedative, antifungal, skin protectant

Phytol
Also found in green tea
Flavors: creamy, earthy, floral, vanilla
Therapeutic effects: anti-insomnia

CANNABACEAE

Hops (used to make beer) and cannabis are both members of the same *Cannabaceae* plant family. Unfortunately hops don't contain any THC but do have similar terpenoids that give pungent beers like IPAs an aroma very similar to marijuana.

CANNABIS FLAVOR PALETTE

The terpenes in cannabis provide a multitude of diverse aroma and flavor profiles. Since taste actually uses the same olfactory senses as smell, we can break down all the main flavors found in cannabis strains into five simple categories: (1) sour, (2) spicy, (3) sweet, (4) bitter, and (5) savory. Each strain has its own unique combination of flavors and this graph breaks down the most common types.

Sweet
CANDY
FLORAL
FRUITY
BERRY
TROPICAL
MINTY

Spicy
EARTHY
WOODY
MUSKY
HERBS
PEPPERY
PINEY

Bitter
ACRID
PUNGENT
SKUNKY
ASTRIGENT
METALLIC

Sour
TART
CITRUS
LEMON
TURPENTINE
FUEL OIL

Savory
OILY
BUTTERY
CHEESEY
CREAMY
DAIRY

Landraces

All of today's strains inevitably derive from pure, ancient cannabis plants found throughout the world and referred to as "landraces." Landraces occur naturally and adapt to a particular region, over a long period of time, without any external influences. Franco Loja from Amsterdam's Green House Seed Co.—the most awarded seed bank in the world—has been traveling the planet in search of these rare landraces with a group known as the Strain Hunters. Following is what Loja has to say:

Why Are Landraces Important?

Cannabis is one of the essential resources of our planet. Landraces represent the most ancient pure form of cannabis we have available, perfected by Mother Nature over hundreds, sometimes over thousands of years, constantly adapting and evolving, improving their harmony with the environment they live in. The plants are larger and generally more vigorous; buds usually form more complex resin that contains more cannabinoids and terpenes. If allowed to develop large in size, these seeds and plants give massive yields. Perhaps most importantly, landraces are the basis for breeding and necessary to creating new and different strains of cannabis.

How Many Different Landrace Varieties Exist?

There are many cannabis landraces almost all over the world. Arjan Roskam, founder of Amsterdam-based Green House Seeds, has been traveling and collecting landraces since the 1980s. He traveled to Southeast Asia to collect landraces in Vietnam, Cambodia, and Laos, and later on to Africa and South America. Since we started the Strain Hunters project, back in 2008, we have collected landraces and documented our travels. We have been to South Africa, Malawi, India, Morocco, Trinidad, St. Vincent and the Grenadines, Jamaica, Swaziland, and more recently to Colombia with the crew from Vice.com.

Are Landraces Mostly Indica or Sativa?

It really varies with the region, but you can say that the only continent on earth where there are true indica landraces is Asia, especially in the Hindu Kush area (Afghanistan, Pakistan, North India, South China). For the rest, landraces in Africa, South America, and Central America are generally sativa; while landraces in Europe and North America are usually low-THC hemp. An exception is North Africa (Morocco) and Central

Durban Poison p/166

Sativa landrace originating from South Africa

Afghani p/56

Indica landrace originating from Afghanistan

Lamb's Bread   p/240

Sativa landrace originating
from Jamaica

Maui Waui   p/258

Sativa landrace originating
from Hawaii

Panama Red   p/288

Sativa landrace originating
from Panama

Asia (Kazakhstan, Armenia, Uzbekistan, Tajikistan, Kyrgyzstan, Azerbaijan, Georgia) where the landraces are the ruderalis variety.

How Do You Know Where to Find Landraces?

Arjan always says, "If you are looking for cannabis, find man first," because man uses cannabis and man propagates cannabis the most, since the beginning of our existence. In most cases the real landraces are found within poor, isolated rural communities in remote areas of third world countries. Landraces are always the dominant plant in their own environment and always overpower any "intrusion." Unfortunately, many landraces are at risk of extinction because of eradication programs or crop-replacement government programs, as it happened in Jamaica and Trinidad. We feel it is our duty to preserve these cannabis landraces for the future of scientific and medical research, and for the basic human right to use a beneficial plant.

What Are the Most Valuable Landraces?

All landraces are valuable, simply because they are plants at risk of being lost forever. Some landraces are more famous than others, and more in demand. The legendary names from the hippy times are still popular today; from the 1970s: Punto Rojo and Colombian Gold, or Malawi Gold, Durban Poison, Limon Verde—these are all very special plants and genetics with a real history.

A history that lives on in pop culture, songs, movies, and through word of mouth passed on from one generation of marijuana smokers to the next.

Why Are Breeding Hybrids So Important?

Mixing genes is always a good thing for the development of any species. This is one of the basic rules of genetics, valid for all forms of complex life on this planet. The thousands of strains available today are the result of over 40 years of breeding in the western world. Cannabis breeding as we know it began on the West Coast of the United States and Canada in the mid-1960s—and it hasn't stopped. It just kept spreading and increasing exponentially. However, there is a need for injecting new genes into the mix. And the best "new" genes are "old" landraces, for the simple reason that they have been inbreeding and selecting themselves on a massive scale for a long period of time.

Buyer's Guide

When it's time to finally part with your hard-earned cash and buy some buds, it's important to know what to look for in order to make sure you're getting your money's worth. If you're able to buy from a legitimate marijuana dispensary then you can trust the weed is going to be stellar. The dispensary's "bud-tender" will be able to detail each strain's specific phenotypes or they will be able to recommend a strain based on your own preferences. But if you're like the majority of recreational smokers, you have to build a trusted network to score some dank nugs. Even still, there's always a chance your regular hookup could have some bad weed from time to time or your budget simply can't afford the best. So here are some important things to examine and rate to determine if the buds make the grade.

LOWS, MIDS, AND HIGHS

Marijuana can be broken down into three quality grades: low, mid or "regs," and high. Here's a quick comparison of the three:

	Low Grade	Mid Grade	High Grade
Bag Appeal	Poor *Lots of extra stems, and seeds*	OK *Some stems and leafs, maybe a few seeds*	Great *No extra stems, leafs, or seeds*
Texture	Dry and compact *Coarse, Seedy lots of shake (crumbs)*	Average *Some buds, some shake*	Full and well-cured *Fluffy dense buds, no shake*
Color	Dull, muddy	Clean, green	Rich, vivid
Flavor	Harsh	Mild	Smooth
THC Content	>1–5%	6–14%	15–25%+
Price	$	$$	$$$

Pedigree

Was the cannabis grown from a reliable source? More often than not, you're going to have to take a leap of faith and take the seller's word. Once you build a strong bond with your source, hopefully they'll share more grow information with you. On the other hand, if you're buying from a dispensary you can always ask them about the genetics, how the cannabis was grown, and other valuable information so you can keep tabs and refer back to the growers or breeders you trust when trying a new strain.

NEW HOOKUPS

When buying from a new source, whether it be a new dispensary or new friend-of-a-friend's source, make sure that at first you buy only a small amount to test their product before purchasing larger amounts the next time around. Any reputable source will respect this gesture and it could save you from wasting your time and money on a bad connection.

Weight

Was the herb prepackaged or was it weighed in front of you? Avoid prepackaged buds and opt for a freshly weighed amount. If you have no choice but to pick a prepackaged baggy, make sure you examine the contents before handing over your money.

Appearance

Do the buds look appealing? At first glance, you should be excited when looking at the bud. It shouldn't be crushed, compressed, or crumbly looking. It should have a nice distinct fluffy nugget shape and the colors—greens, reds, and/or purple hues—can be light or dark and should look clean and vibrant,

not dull and dirty. The bud should also look nicely manicured, meaning all the bigger leaves and extra stems trimmed off nicely; not left on or hacked away.

TRICHOMES

Can you see tiny crystals all over the bud? Your buds should have plenty of clear or amber-tinted resin crystals if you expect to get the most effects from it. Ideally, it will be glistening with crystals but sometimes storing and moving can cause some to fall off, which isn't a big deal. But if they are seen in odd patches, or there are only a few crystals, or none at all then the herb was not properly taken care of and you shouldn't pay top dollar for it.

Feel

How does the bud feel when you touch it? Properly dried and cured buds should be neither dry nor wet; neither rock-solid nor brittle. The bud should feel dense and squishy. When you break it up, it should be easy to grind and feel sticky. It shouldn't crumble into a fine powder (too dry) or clump into hard balls (too wet). Any stems should bend then break when bent, not just bend without breaking or quickly snap off.

Smell

Does it smell appealing? The aromas should be pleasant and appetizing to you. Chances are if you like the way it smells, you'll love the way it tastes. Just keep in mind that smell has nothing to do with potency, just flavor. Some of the best and strongest buds can smell very harsh and even skunk-like or can just have a slight, subtle fragrance. One exception is if the buds smell very "green"—sort of like fresh lawn clippings—then it probably wasn't

cured properly and won't be tasty or potent. The other is if it smells "dirty."

DIRTY WEED

Sometimes improperly grown or stored weed can grow mold and/or mildew. If the bud smells moldy, very muddy, or like ammonia, then chances are it has mold. If you see white stringy stuff or an unnatural white coating on the exterior, that's definitely a sign of mold or mildew. Both of these are bad signs and you shouldn't buy it, never mind smoke it.

Personal Experience

How did it make you feel? Above all else, this is the most important factor to consider when buying bud. This is a very personal preference that only you can experience, so it's worth taking notes and keeping a journal on which strains you've tried, where you bought them, and what you enjoyed (or didn't enjoy) about them so you can start appreciating and recognizing all the wonderful and distinct experiences various strains have to offer.

THE NEGATIVE EFFECTS

New users and experienced smokers alike might sometimes experience a few negative effects after toking a new strain. Don't panic, these minor side effects are temporary and should wear off quickly, so just relax and let the time pass. If they mess with your high, stop using that strain and try a new variety next time.

DRY MOUTH
HEADACHE
PARANOIA
DIZZINESS
DRY EYES
CONFUSION

100 Bona Fide Cannabis Terms

Using code words for marijuana has always been commonplace among stoners. The word "marijuana" or "marihuana" became popular in the 1930s when our federal government literally made up this exotic sounding name for cannabis in an attempt to scare the public and vilify its use. As with all things related to cannabis, our government got it completely wrong and this most popular name has been embraced and adopted by potheads worldwide. The Office of National Drug Control Policy has since issued a shocking 647 official "street names" for marijuana and once again failed (does anyone really call it "dinkie dow"?!). So, here is a list of acceptable A–Z terms with more positive vibes. Use these for your own personal enjoyment or as inspiration when creating your own cannabis code.

1 420
2 Atshitshi
3 Beasters
4 Bhang
5 Bo (Bobo)
6 Bomb
7 Boo
8 Boom
9 Broccoli
10 Bubonic
11 Bud
12 Buddha
13 Bush
14 Cest
15 Cheeba
16 Cheech
17 Chicken
18 Choke
19 Chronic
20 Coli
21 Dagga
22 Dank
23 Dew
24 Doobie (Doob, Dube)
25 Dope
26 Dro

27 Elephant
28 Endo
29 Esra
30 Fire
31 Flower
32 Funk
33 Ganja (Ganj, Ghanja, Gunga, Ganga)
34 Giggle
35 Goofy
36 Grass
37 Green
38 Haze
39 Headies
40 Hemp
41 Herb
42 Homegrown
43 Hooch
44 Hoot (Hooter)
45 Hydro
46 Indo
47 Jane
48 Jolly
49 Joy
50 Kali
51 Kaya

52 KGB
53 Killer
54 Kind
55 Kush
56 Ladies
57 Leaf
58 Lettuce
59 Loud
60 Love
61 Lye
62 Mary Jane (Mary, Aunt Mary, M.J.)
63 Meds (Medicine)
64 Meg (Meggie)
65 Mooca (Moocha)
66 Mota
67 Noog
68 Nugs (Nuggets)
69 Number
70 Pakalolo
71 Pot
72 Puff
73 Purps (Purple)
74 Queen Ann
75 Reefer
76 Rope

77 Salad
78 Sess
79 Shway
80 Sinsemilla
81 Skunk
82 Smoke
83 Stank
84 Sticky (Icky)
85 Stuff
86 Tea
87 Toke
88 Treats
89 Trees
90 Tweed
91 Uno
92 Viper (Vipe, Vape)
93 Wacky (Tobaccy)
94 Weed
95 Wheat
96 Wool
97 X.L.
98 Yerba
99 Yesca (Yesco)
100 Zambi

NEGATIVE TERMS

Brick
Bunk
Dirt
Ditch
Schwag
Sticks

ANCIENT TERMS

Chuma China
Ganjika India
Kaneh Bosm Hebrew
Kánnabis Greek
Kanubi Sumarian
Qunabu Mesopotamia

Quantity Terms

One of the easiest choices you can make when procuring your marijuana is the actual amount you want. The most important thing to remember is how many grams are in each amount so you don't get shorted. Here's a rundown of the standard weights available to purchase along with their common "code" names.

Gram (1 gram)

A.K.A. *dub, g, grizz, piece, sock*

⅛ Ounce (3.5 grams)

A.K.A. *eighth, eighter, sack, single, slice, shirt*

¼ Ounce (7 grams)

A.K.A. *bottle, pants, q, quad, quarter*

½ Ounce (14 grams)

A.K.A. *half, half-o, halfer, halfie*

¾ Ounce (21 grams)

A.K.A. *lid*

1 Ounce (28 grams)

A.K.A. *jacket, onion, oscar, o, o.z., oz, ozzy, zip, zone*

¼ Pound (4 ounces)

A.K.A. *40's, cutie pie, q. p., quop*

½ Pound (8 ounces)

A.K.A. *h. p., half-p*

1 Pound (16 ounces)

A.K.A. *elbow, p*

Money Terms

Sometimes you can buy weed for a dollar amount rather than weight. These are typically "eye balled" amounts and aren't the best quality chronic.

Nickel (worth $5)

Should be enough for a joint.
A.K.A. *fives, nick, nickel bag*

Dime (worth $10)

Should be enough for a blunt.
A.K.A. *dime bag, dime sack, ten*

Dub (worth $20)

Should be enough for two blunts—i.e., double.
A.K.A. *dub, dub sack, twin, twenty*

Keep It Fresh

Properly storing your buds is crucial to keeping them fresh, flavorful, and potent for a long time. Excess light, heat, and humidity will damage the weed and diminish its potency. Poor storage is what makes good buds go bad but thankfully it's pretty easy to keep them fresh and sticky.

SHELF LIFE

Properly stored marijuana will stay fresh and potent for months on end losing only around 5–10% of its potency annually, while improperly stored marijuana can lose much of its value and potency within a few short weeks.

No Bags

Plastic sandwich "baggies" were not intended for storing your buds, they're just a cheap and easy way to package them for selling. Baggies not only dry out your buds, they won't protect your buds from getting crushed, and the plastic also causes a static that attracts and pulls crystals away from the buds. Make sure you transfer your buds into a proper container as soon as you can.

Airtight

To store your herb, an airtight glass jar is best. You can use a simple mason jar with a screw-top lid or invest in one designed specifically for weed. Even a small Tupperware-like container or a prescription pill bottle will work. Either way, make sure the container is airtight and the appropriate size. You don't want a jar that's too big with a lot of extra air trapped inside and you don't want to crush and cram the buds into the container to fit.

Handling

Too much handling will cause the crystals to fall off so don't fool around with your nugs other than pulling them out from the jar right before you're ready to use them. Also, make sure to avoid constantly opening and closing your containers—air will dry out your buds. And never add any extra moisture to your weed, including peels from fruits or vegetables. This can cause bacteria and mold to grow and ruin your stash.

Storage

Store your nug jar indoors in a cool, dry, and dark place. A simple drawer or cabinet will do the trick. You just don't want your stored buds in temperatures below 40 degrees Fahrenheit and above 80 degrees Fahrenheit and you definitely don't want the temperature to fluctuate all the time. Also, avoid refrigerating or freezing your buds. Constant changes in the refrigerator's humidity levels is a major problem and freezing temperatures will actually cause all the trichome crystals to freeze up and break off the bud.

Bud and Beyond

Buds are the most popular and widespread choice when it comes to buying and consuming cannabis. Aside from buds, cannabis can also be made into a variety of other potent products in the forms of concentrates and edibles. Following is an overview of the variety readily available.

Natural Forms

Cannabis as Mother Nature intended—natural, pure, and unprocessed.

Raw

Freshly cut flowers from the plant can be eaten raw. Although it requires very large quantities, some therapeutic effects can result, but any psychoactive effect is diminished.

Buds

The ripe flowers are harvested from the plant, precisely manicured, and then dry cured to produce wonderful buds ready to enjoy. Proper drying and curing is essential to lock in potency while enhancing the overall flavor and aroma of the bud. Buds are ultimately enjoyed in a multitude of smoking and vaporizing options (see *Smoking Options*, page 36).

Kief

Kief is another word for the trichome crystals that have fallen off or have been manually sifted from the leaves and flowers using a screen. Kief is a raw powder form and can be added to buds when smoking, or can be compressed into balls or blocks called pressed kief or hashish.

DECARBOXYLATION

All forms of cannabis need to be heated, burned, ignited, or vaporized at some point in order to activate its chemical compounds. This activation of cannabinoids is called decarboxylation. In other words, without the heat you won't get high.

Concentrates

Concentrates are cannabis products made by extracting the cannabinoids and terpenes from the plant using a variety of mechanical extraction processes. The resulting "extractions" are comprised of 60–90% THC content and are the most potent forms of cannabis available—getting you much higher, much quicker.

Hash

Using a cold ice water extraction technique, trichome resins become separated and isolated from the plant material through a filtration system. The filtered material is then compressed into a final cake form. Hash's quality is dependent on the proportion of plant material to trichomes, the less plant material the better. These varying qualities can be visually measured when the hash is heated—it will either "bubble" or "melt."

Bubble Hash

It contains the most plant material of all the hash varieties and thus "bubbles" when first lit. If it bubbles throughout the entire heating process, it is called Full Bubble.

Half Melt Hash

It contains less plant material than Full Bubble Hash. Half Melt Hash will melt at first and then turn into a gooey matter as it continues to heat.

Full Melt Hash

This is the highest quality of all hash. Made up of mostly pure trichomes, Full Melt contains only trace amounts of plant material—leaving very little to no residue after it's heated.

Oil

Oil, sometimes called "hash oil" or "wax," is made using a complex extraction process that involves lab equipment, heat, vacuums, and solvents like alcohol, butane, or carbon dioxide (CO_2) to extract the trichome resins from the plant. Most waxes are extracted using butane and are commonly referred to as BHO (butane hash oil or butane honey oil). Oils can come in many different colors, shapes, and sizes depending on the strain used, type of solvent, purging method, and the overall consistency. Following are some of the most common types you'll run into.

Shatter

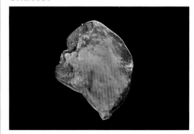

Shatter, sometimes called "glass," has a consistency similar to hard candy or glass. It gets its name because it often shatters like glass when a piece is broken off. *Other terms: amber glass, glass, sap*

Wax

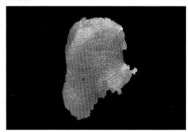

Wax has a consistency similar to modeling clay. This form is very popular since it is fairly easy to handle and vaporize. *Other term: earwax*

Continued on next page

Concentrates (continued)

Budder

Budder is very sticky and is created by whipping the wax after the solvent has been purged off. Whipping aerates the oil and gives it a cloudier appearance. The end result has a similar look and texture to peanut butter.
Other term: taffy (a glossier version of budder)

Crumble

Crumble has a dry, crumbly texture similar to brown sugar, making it very easy to handle.

Honeycomb

Very similar to crumble, but during the purging process, air bubbles form inside the wax due to low purging heat. The wax doesn't melt and the air pockets don't collapse, leaving small holes throughout.
Other term: moonrocks

QWISO

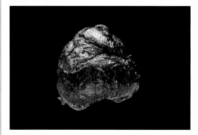

Quick wash isopropyl alcohol hash oil (QWISO) is a way to make hash oil without using butane or carbon dioxide gases. Ground buds are soaked in isopropyl alcohol for a short time. A filter is then used to separate the alcohol from the plant material and the filtered alcohol is left to evaporate off, leaving behind your QWISO.

710

While the code term 420 is synonymous with smoking buds, the term 710 is code for dabbing oils—710 upside down spells O-I-L.

DABBING

Although concentrates can be added to your bud when smoking, concentrates are most often used alone and vaporized by using a torch to heat a titanium or glass element. The concentrate is then applied or "dabbed" onto the hot surface, vaporizing the concentrate instantly. The resulting vapor is usually filtered through a water pipe. Glass bongs and bubblers that are made for concentrate use are called "oil rigs."

DON'T OVER EAT

When smoking marijuana the effects can be felt almost instantly, within minutes. When enjoying edibles, it can take up to one hour to feel anything. The effects gradually increase as the body digests the edible. This long digestion makes it very hard to judge how much you should actually eat and also produces a much longer-lasting and stronger body high compared to other forms of marijuana.

NO NEWBIES

If you are a new or inexperienced user of marijuana, kief, concentrates and edibles are not good options to experiment with. These forms are very potent and are recommended for experienced and veteran users only.

Edibles

Enjoying foods and drinks infused with cannabis is a tasty alternative to smoking. Popular cannabis edibles include brownies, cookies, cakes, cupcakes, fudge, caramels, and lollipops. Since heat is necessary to activate the THC and other cannabinoids, simply grinding up your weed and adding it to a recipe will give you very little psychoactive results. The key component to edibles is either cooking your cannabis or creating a cooking butter or oil infused with THC that is then used in your recipes to create the edible of your choice.

Canna-butter

By slowly cooking finely ground up buds and leaves with dairy butter you extract and transfer the THC and cannabinoid oils into the butter.

Oil

The same process can be used to make cooking oils, olive oil, canola oil, or vegetable oil and can also be infused with THC and cannabinoid oils.

Tea

A cannabis tea can be made by boiling ground buds in water and adding cream or milk to make the THC more soluble.

Tincture

An alcoholic extract, decarboxylated buds and leaves are soaked in a high-proof alcohol spirit. The resulting liquid is then consumed by placing a few drops on your tongue or by adding to recipes and drinks.

Salve

By melting cannabis infused oil with beeswax you can create a topical cream that can be applied to the skin.

Smoking Options

The legendary Bob Marley once said, "When you smoke the herb, it reveals you to yourself." Smoking is and always has been the most common way to enjoy marijuana—dating back thousands of years across many different cultures worldwide. Smoking herb is also a social activity, done communally among friends old or new, passing, sharing, and bonding over a common experience. In today's cannabis culture, there's an assortment of tools and methods used to light it up.

Joint

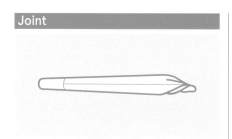

A joint is literally a marijuana cigarette, ground-up bud twisted in a rolling paper, and one of the most popular ways herb is smoked. Joints are relatively easy to roll (see *How to Roll*, page 40) and even easier to pass around. They're also great for customizing based on how much weed you add—from an oversized "doobie" to a thin "pinner."

Spliff

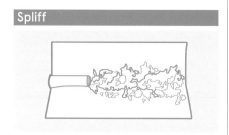

A spliff is nearly identical to a joint except loose tobacco is mixed in with the herb before rolling. Many spliffs are rolled in a cone or bat shape and are very popular in Europe. If you're smoking with others, it is customary to let them know your spliff contains tobacco before passing to them. In Jamaica the term "spliff" refers to a regular joint containing no tobacco.

Blunt

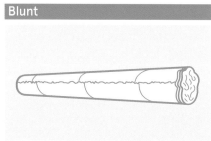

Blunts are ground buds rolled in the outer tobacco leaf wrapping of a cigar or prepackaged "blunt wraps." Compared to joints, blunts are much larger, burn much slower, and can be passed around many more times. The tobacco wrapping does affect the overall flavor of the herb but is still a preferred method by many experienced smokers, who take great pride in how well they can roll them. "Blunted" is a term used to describe how one feels after smoking a blunt.

PREPARING BUDS

Breaking up your weed is a labor of love and an important step in any smoking process. Pulling the sticky buds away from the stem (and occasional seed) and breaking up the bud is key to an even burn and smooth smoking experience. Simply use your fingers, sharp scissors, or buy a special marijuana grinder to get the job done.

Pipes

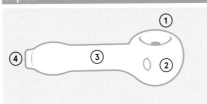

Pipes are relatively small, easy to use, and well suited to be passed around, making them a popular smoking tool. Often called a "bowl," pipes are traditionally made out of a variety of materials including glass, metal, wood, stone, corncob, or even homemade out of apples or aluminum cans. The overall best bowls for smoking herb are handblown glass. Your standard pipe consists of:

① **BOWL:** to hold the herb
② **CARB:** A side opening (carburator) used to control air flow
③ **STEM:** to collect the smoke
④ **MOUTHPIECE:** to hold against your lips

Simply pack, light, and inhale. When holding the pipe around the bowl, make sure to cover the carb while lighting the herb. Opening the carb allows for more airflow and is done to clear all the smoke from the stem as you finish taking your hit. Pipes also come in a variety of shapes and sizes, such as the following:

One Hitter

A one hitter or a "bat" is a small, discreet pipe that only holds enough weed for a single hit. They are very convenient to transport, conceal, and easy to use.

Chillum

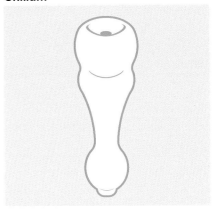

This straight pipe is open on both ends and smoked upright through cupped hands so as not to touch your lips. Although they take some practice to use, chillums provide one of the strongest hits you can get from a pipe.

Bubbler

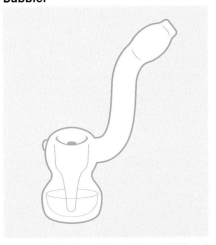

A bubbler is a glass pipe with an additional chamber that holds a small amount of water—and it is referred to as a water pipe. The smoke is filtered through the water chamber to offer a much smoother hit than other dry pipes.

Bong

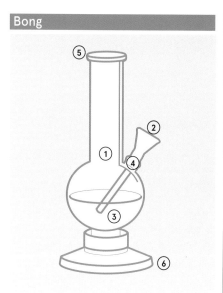

A bong is technically a water pipe, but in the form of a larger, upright stand-alone unit with a much more sophisticated anatomy. A bong is made up of the following parts:

(1) CHAMBER: holds the water and collects the smoke

(2) BOWL: to hold the buds

(3) SLIDE: the "male" unit that the bowl is attached to

(4) DOWNSTEM: the "stem" or "female" unit that the slide inserts into

(5) MOUTHPIECE: used to draw and fill the chamber with smoke

(6) BASE: to keep the bong steady when not in use

To hit a bong, light the bud, and inhale from the mouthpiece. Once the chamber, is full, the bowl and slide are pulled out of the downstem as you continue to inhale. With the downstem now open, air will release the smoke from the chamber causing it to rush into your lungs and making for a big hit. Always place the bong down on its base when you're done.

Hookah

Like a bong, a hookah is a freestanding water pipe except it has multiple, flexible hoses extending from its large base unit. The smoke is filtered through the water and then out through the hoses where multiple smokers can simultaneously draw steady long hits at a leisurely pace.

Vaporizers

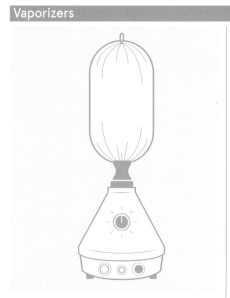

Vaporizing has become a popular modern method for consuming high-grade herbs. Unlike all the other smoking methods, vaporizers do not involve ignition. Instead, vaporizers use electricity to heat herb to just below the point of combustion; emitting a "vapor" that is smoke free and consisting mainly of pure cannabinoids and terpenes. Vaporizers come is many forms from tabletop plug-in units, portable battery powered handhelds, or even adapters that fit traditional water pipes.

Forrest Landry, inventor of the famed Magic-Flight Launch Box Vaporizer, explains why vaporizing has become so popular:

Cleaner Than Smoking
Vaporized herb has little to no smell with no tars or any other by-products from traditional smoking methods. You're also not burning or consuming any plant matter, including chlorophyll or cellulose. You are just inhaling pure cannabinoids and terpenes.

Better Flavor Profiles
Vaporization is going to be far more honest as to what the truth of the plant is than smoking ever can be. Because the body of the plant is being heated up more sequentially, more evenly, the lighter flavor components will tend to come off in a body, as a group, and you'll have the experience of sensing all the terpenes' nuances and honest flavors.

Requires Less Herb
Since vapor consists of 95% pure cannabinoids there is very little waste making for optimal use of your herb. Your supply can last up to four times longer.

A Clearer Experience
You will have a clearer, cleaner, more euphoric experience since you're not absorbing any of the other by-products from combusted smoke. Also, the components that are being released have lower volatilization temperatures and tend to have more euphoric characteristics.

How to Roll

Rolling a perfect joint is a rite of passage for any true smoker. Even if you prefer other smoking methods, knowing how to roll is still a necessary skill to master.

What You Need

To roll a perfect joint, you'll need between ½ to 1 gram of your favorite strain (ground up), a rolling paper, and a crutch.

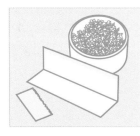

WHY THE CRUTCH?

1. It gives the joint structure.
2. It makes the joint easier to roll.
3. You don't get weed in your mouth.
4. No roach clip needed at the end.

Step 1

You can make the crutch, or mouth piece, out of any thick, cardboard-like paper.

★ A good choice is to rip off a piece of the rolling paper packaging, or find a business card to use, or use actual filter paper.

Roll the crutch into a tight cylinder.

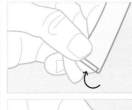

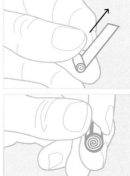

Step 2

Lay the crutch in the paper with about ¼ of it hanging off of the end.

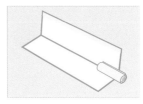

Make sure the paper's glue strip is facing you. Now put your ground bud in the paper.

Spread it out with your fingers until it's even. Now we're ready to start rolling.

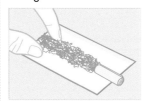

Step 3

Fold the paper and hold the joint by the crutch—make sure the glue strip is at the top.

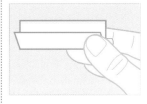

Then with your other hand, pinch the paper together above the bud and gently start rolling, moving evenly towards the center and then outwards.

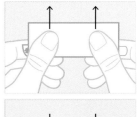

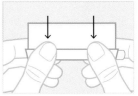

★ It's best to let your thumbs do the work while your fingers support the joint itself.

Step ④

Continue rolling evenly back and forth until the bud holds its cylindrical shape on its own.

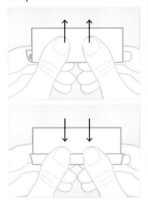

If your bud isn't too dry, when you lay the joint flat it should hold its cylindrical shape.

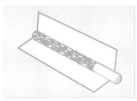

★ Just make sure it's not compressed too tightly, otherwise the joint will be too hard to hit and/or won't stay lit.

Step ⑤

Now comes the hardest part, the tuck. Roll the paper down so that the long end is away from you.

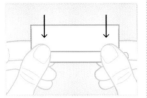

Now use your thumbs to press the short end of the paper into the gap between the long end of the paper and the crutch. As you press it in, you can use your pointer finger to guide the short end of the paper under the long one.

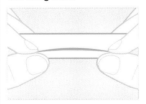

Continue rolling until you only have a little bit left. Then lick the paper.

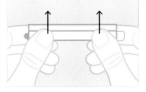

Step ⑥

Starting at the tip and working your way to the crutch, seal the joint.

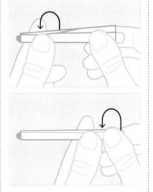

Finish off the joint by packing down the bud in the open end using a poker, like a pen or pencil.

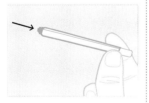

Lastly, push the crutch into the bottom end until it's flush; this helps to ensure that the material at the base of the joint gets packed tightly.

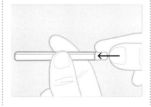

Final Step

Spark it up and enjoy your creation.

Smoking Etiquette

Sharing pot has been ingrained within the cannabis culture since the very beginning. It's what brings us together and what allows us to not only share our herb, but also share our ideas, stories, laughter, and good times. Proper etiquette or "headiquette" dictates that a set of good manners be practiced as a sign of respect to the herb and to the friends we're about to enjoy it with.

Puff and Give

"Puff. . .Puff. . .Pass" when smoking a joint, spliff, or blunt and "Puff. . .Pass" when smoking other paraphernalia. This golden rule will ensure that everyone gets to smoke an equal amount and keeps the rotation moving.

Keep the Rotation

It's common practice to pass to your left-hand side but whichever way the rotation starts make sure you stay with the same rotation until everyone has had a turn. Just don't "bogart" or take forever to take your hits, even if it's your weed. Take your puffs and keep the rotation moving.

Take the First Hit

The person who rolls or packs (no matter whose weed it is) gets the option to light up the first hit, or they can give the honor to another person of their choice. The first hit is often referred to as getting "greens."

Leave Green Hits

When smoking from a bowl, try not to torch all the green in the bowl. With the right lighting angle you can burn half or a third of the green and be able to pass another fresh "green hit" for the next person to enjoy. This is known as "cornering" the bowl.

Keep It Dry

Don't slobber or drool on whatever it is you are smoking from; no one likes to take a hit from a wet blunt or slobbering mouthpiece. And if you're sick, never take a hit from something others are going to smoke from too.

Cashed Out

If after you hit a bowl you think that all of the weed has been smoked and the bowl is pretty much empty, it is common courtesy to tell the person you are passing to that you believe it may be "cashed."

Enough for Everyone

Make sure you break up enough weed for everyone in the circle to have at least one hit. If a bowl's been cashed before everyone has had a hit, make sure you pack some more and give it back to the proper person in the rotation.

Join In

If you're trying to join a session that's already begun, don't just cut in. Always ask the group if it's okay to join and where you should wait in the rotation.

Don't Hit and Run

Always try to stay in the group until the session is over. Never take a hit and immediately leave.

Return the Favor

You should do your best to reciprocate if you can. Don't always be the guy showing up with no smoke. If you have some bud, always ask to contribute to the session or offer to use it for the next session.

Keep It Private

Unless you're close friends, don't ask how much another person's nugs cost, or where and if you can buy some. If you really want to know, pull them aside after the session and ask them in private.

House Rules

If you're at someone else's place, make sure you ask the host if it's okay to smoke and where they prefer it happen, and make sure to ask them if they want to join.

Good Hook ups

If a friend hooks you up with some herb, it is common courtesy to offer them the opportunity to smoke some at the exchange.

Lights Out

Don't ever let a lit joint or blunt go out because you were talking too much or "politic-ing" or just spaced out. If you're too high or are in a serious conversation just step out of the rotation.

Never Pocket a Lighter

At the end of a session, don't keep the lighter if it's not yours. Always make an effort to give it back to its owner.

Respect Others

Never blow smoke in anyone's face, don't peer pressure anyone into smoking if they don't want to, and never complain or talk down about other people's weed. If you don't like it, don't smoke it. But if someone has dank buds, or even rolls a nice joint or blunt, it's appropriate to give a nice compliment.

Myths and Misconceptions

Marijuana prohibitionists have been using false propaganda, misinformation, and flawed study results in an attempt to influence drug policy and manipulate the general public into thinking marijuana is bad for you. One only need watch the 1936 film *Reefer Madness* to understand this idiocy. But is pot really bad for you? Julie Holland, MD, editor of *The Pot Book*, is part of a new generation of researchers helping to debunk these myths and redefine the role of cannabis in today's world.

MYTH
Cannabis Is a Schedule I Drug

Julie Holland, MD:
The United States has taken out a patent on the use of cannabis as a neuroprotectant, though they continue to keep the plant in Schedule I, reserved for drugs with the highest potential for abuse and no medicinal use. Groups of physicians and nurses, including the American Medical Association, have requested a review of this scheduling. And THC pills, which can get you extremely altered, are listed in Schedule III. It makes no sense to list the whole plant in Schedule I when one compound of the plant is available by prescription in the same safety category as Xanax and Vicodin.

It is very difficult to perform Schedule I research in any institution, but the truth is, it's easier to get permission to give heroin or cocaine or methylenedioxymethamphetamine (MDMA) to research subjects than it is to get our government to release cannabis for therapeutic studies. Because the government will not allow, never mind fund therapeutic studies, and big pharma isn't very well going to help either, clinical research depends on private donations for sustenance.

MYTH
Cannabis Kills Brain Cells and Destroys Your Memory

Julie Holland, MD:
Cannabis is nontoxic to the brain. It in no way kills brain cells, and it has been proven to be neuroprotective, that is, sparing brain cells that are exposed to toxins or lack of oxygen.

While you are intoxicated with cannabis you have diminished working memory, but once the drug wears off your memory returns intact.

MYTH

Cannabis Is a Gateway Drug

Julie Holland, MD:
There has never been convincing evidence of cannabis being a gateway drug, but there are some anecdotal reports of alcoholics as well as heroin and cocaine addicts being maintained on cannabis instead of their more toxic drug of choice. Also, there is new evidence that CBD may help people quit smoking cigarettes.

MYTH

Cannabis Is Highly Addictive

Julie Holland, MD:
While a minority of people can become addicted to cannabis (and others can become addicted to gambling, or to Facebook, or internet porn) most people who use cannabis do not become addicted. Among cigarettes, heroin, cocaine, alcohol, and cannabis, the rates of addiction are lowest for cannabis (and highest for cigarettes). Also, the withdrawal syndrome for cannabis is mild and short-lived. Alcohol withdrawal is potentially deadly.

MYTH

Cannabis Has No Medical Value

Julie Holland, MD:
Cannabis is an ancient medicine that has been used for millennia to treat insomnia, anxiety, menstrual cramps, nausea, and loss of appetite. It is the oldest known domesticated plant and plant medicine, with medicinal texts from 2,000 and 3,000 years ago mentioning the plant. It was listed in the U.S. Pharmacopeia until the 1940s.

Just because you make a drug illegal doesn't strip it of its medicinal properties.

THC is a Food and Drug Administration (FDA)–approved drug to treat nausea and pain. Sativex (an extract of THC and CBD) is approved in forty countries to treat muscle spasms of Multiple Sclerosis. Oncologists worldwide recommend cannabis to fight the side effects of chemotherapy, and in a recent survey, 70% of doctors would recommend medicinal cannabis to a patient who could benefit from it.

Through proper education and research people can be educated to change their views on pot, will avail themselves of medicinal cannabis and also choose a drug for recreation that is less toxic and more health-sustaining than alcohol, cigarettes, or many other commonly used substances.

NORML Principles of Responsible Use

When marijuana is enjoyed responsibly, subjecting users to harsh criminal and civil penalties provides no public benefit and causes terrible injustices. The oldest and largest marijuana legalization organization in the country, National Organization for the Reform of Marijuana Laws (NORML) has provided a voice in the public policy debate for those Americans who oppose marijuana prohibition and favor an end to the practice of arresting marijuana smokers. For reasons of public safety, public health, economics, and justice, the prohibition laws should be repealed to the extent that they criminalize responsible cannabis use. By adoption of this statement, the NORML Board of Directors has attempted to define "responsible cannabis use."

I. Adults Only

Cannabis consumption is for adults only. It is irresponsible to provide cannabis to children.

Many things and activities are suitable for young people, but others absolutely are not. Children do not drive cars, enter into contracts, or marry, and they must not use drugs. As it is unrealistic to demand lifetime abstinence from cars, contracts, and marriage, however, it is unrealistic to expect lifetime abstinence from all intoxicants, including alcohol. Rather, our expectation and hope for young people is that they grow up to be responsible adults. Our obligation to them is to demonstrate what that means.

II. No Driving

The responsible cannabis consumer does not operate a motor vehicle or other dangerous machinery while impaired by cannabis, nor (like other responsible citizens) while impaired by any other substance or condition, including some medicines and when fatigued.

Although the use of cannabis is said by most experts to be safer than alcohol and many prescription drugs, responsible cannabis consumers never operate motor vehicles in an impaired condition. Public safety demands not only that impaired drivers be taken off the road, but that objective measures of impairment be developed and used, rather than chemical testing.

III. Set and Setting

The responsible cannabis user will carefully consider the set and setting, regulating use accordingly.

"Set" refers to the consumer's values, attitudes, experience, and personality; and "setting" means the consumer's physical and social circumstances. The responsible cannabis consumer will be vigilant as to conditions—time, place, mood, etc.— and does not hesitate to say "no" when those conditions are not conducive to a safe, pleasant, and/or productive experience.

IV. Resist Abuse

Use of cannabis, to the extent that it impairs health, personal development, or achievement, is abuse, to be resisted by responsible cannabis users.

Abuse means harm. Some cannabis use is harmful; most is not. That which is harmful should be discouraged. Wars have been waged in the name of eradicating "drug abuse," but instead of focusing on abuse, enforcement measures have been diluted by targeting all drug use, whether abusive or not. If cannabis abuse is to be targeted, it is essential that clear standards be developed to identify it.

V. Respect Rights of Others

The responsible cannabis user does not violate the rights of others, observes accepted standards of courtesy and public propriety, and respects the preferences of those who wish to avoid cannabis entirely.

No one may violate the rights of others, and no substance use excuses any such violation. Regardless of the legal status of cannabis, responsible users will adhere to emerging tobacco smoking protocols in public and private places.

BUDS

Cannabis Strains

Marijuana has come a long way since the days of our ancestors. Today, creative minds across the world are cultivating and crossbreeding cannabis plants to create modern-day marvels in the form of majestically beautiful and one-of-a-kind strains—from heirloom landraces to creatively named super hybrids. The following pages will guide you through some of the best varieties of marijuana strains we could find, organized alphabetically by strain name. While the breathtaking focus-stacked images will give you a high-definition visual of their appearance, the profile information will provide you with the unique details specific to each individual strain. Each profile includes the following:

STRAIN NAME
The name given to the strain by the original breeder or grower.

TYPE
The strain's variety—
sativa ● (100%)
sativa hybrid ● (> 60% sativa)
hybrid ● (≈ 50% sativa + 50% indica)
indica hybrid ● (> 60% indica)
indica ● (100%)

LINEAGE
The genetic female and male parents.

SMELL/TASTE
The common aromas and flavors.

COMMON EFFECTS
The common physical and psychoactive effects.

TOP MEDICINAL USES
Conditions the strain has been known to help.

AWARDS
Any major awards received (1st, 2nd, or 3rd place).

SIMILAR STRAINS
Other strains that share similar phenotypes.

DESCRIPTION
A brief outline of other pertinent information about the strain.

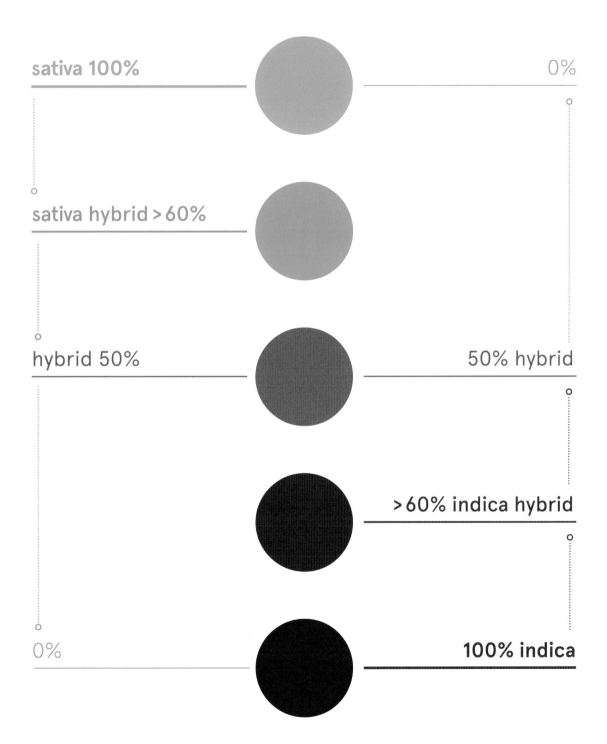

sativa 100%   0%

sativa hybrid > 60%

hybrid 50%   50% hybrid

>60% indica hybrid

0%   **100% indica**

STRAIN NAME

5Gs × OGSD ●

TYPE
hybrid ●

LINEAGE
(Dieselberry × Witches Weed) ×
(OG Kush × Sour Diesel)

SMELL/TASTE
lemon, acrid, fuel

COMMON EFFECTS
uplifted, creative, euphoria

TOP MEDICINAL USES
mood enhancement, stress

SIMILAR STRAINS
Chemdawg ● p/132
Allen Wrench ● p/66
NYC Diesel ● p/274

This unique breed hails from the infamous Humboldt County region of California—well regarded as the birthplace of modern-day hybrid cannabis cultivation. This strain consists of elite genetics combined with great breeding skills to produce a nice one-off hybrid that's as potent as it is stinky. The dense buds have a very lemony aroma and flavor, mixed with a fuel funk and a dash of sour orange zest. Overall, 5Gs × OGSD is a prime example of a Humboldt original.

STRAIN NAME

Abusive OG ●

TYPE
hybrid ●

LINEAGE
OG Kush phenotype

SMELL/TASTE
lemon, pine, fuel

COMMON EFFECTS
cheerful, uplifted, relaxed

TOP MEDICINAL USES
mood enhancement, anxiety

SIMILAR STRAINS
SFV OG ● p/324
Tahoe OG ● p/368
XXX OG ● p/390

This variety of the renowned OG Kush is rumored to have origins that trace back to the famous rap artist and marijuana advocate Snoop Dogg. Regardless of the rumors, Abusive OG is no doubt a prime example of an OG—very dense nugs heavily coated in crystals with a unique sour pine flavor commonly referred to as "kushy." These buds' ability to deliver a long–lasting, body-buzzing high is what makes Abusive OG a cut above the rest.

The Legend of OG

When "OG" is used in a strain name, it typically refers to its lineage back to the original OG Kush strain. The initials OG are thought by most to mean "Ocean Grown" for OG Kush's roots in Southern California, while some attribute OG to mean "Original Gangster" to represent the first generation of a strain. Semantics aside, OG strains are widely popular and highly coveted for their distinct flavors, appearance, and enduring effects.

STRAIN NAME

Afghani ●

TYPE
indica ●

LINEAGE
Landrace (Afghanistan)

SMELL/TASTE
spicy, citrus, earthy

COMMON EFFECTS
body buzz, sleepy, couch-lock

TOP MEDICINAL USES
insomnia, pain

SIMILAR STRAINS
G-13 ● p/176
Sour Bubble ● p/336
Purple Sticky Punch ● p/312

Afghani is known throughout the world as one of the finest pure indica cannabis strains. Its dark sticky flowers are a fast and easy grow and its monsterous resin production and trademark indica effects make it an indispensable component in the breeding of many other famous hybrid strains. The mellow, exotic flavors smoke smooth and hit strong. A favorite nighttime strain, Afghani's ability to produce long-lasting and body-numbing physical effects is second to none.

STRAIN NAME

Afgoo ●

TYPE
indica hybrid ●

LINEAGE
Afghani × Maui Haze

SMELL/TASTE
piney, spicy, strawberry

COMMON EFFECTS
mellow, sleepy, euphoria

TOP MEDICINAL USES
insomnia, pain

SIMILAR STRAINS
Strawberry Cough ● p/352
Maui Waui ● p/258
Afwreck ● p/60

———

This supersticky bud blends two legendary landrace strains to create a very effective and powerful indica-dominant stunner. The smoke is earthy flavored with subtle hints of sweet strawberry, and the heavy full-body high can be felt almost as soon as you exhale—and then it seems to last forever. Newcomers to Afgoo may experience a couch-lock effect with this perfect nighttime treat. A hint of euphoria will also creep in (thanks to its Maui Haze genetics), making Afgoo a great smoke to end a long, hard day.

STRAIN NAME

Afwreck

TYPE
sativa hybrid ●

LINEAGE
Afghani × Trainwreck

SMELL/TASTE
sweet, floral, citrus

COMMON EFFECTS
uplifting, euphoria, cheerful

TOP MEDICINAL USES
stress, mood enhancement

SIMILAR STRAINS
Afgoo ● p/58
J1 ● p/220
Cherry AK ● p/136

———

Although crossed with Afghani, Afwreck's phenotypes have been influenced mostly from its powerful Trainwreck parent. This strong sativa has a pleasant mix of sweet and sour flavors that are balanced with a fresh floral aroma. The effects immediately focus exclusively on the mind while the Afghani makes a late guest appearance to add a subtle body high that finishes off the buzz nicely.

STRAIN NAME

Agent Orange ●

TYPE
hybrid ●

LINEAGE
Orange Velvet × Jack the Ripper

SMELL/TASTE
citrus, orange, sour

COMMON EFFECTS
cheerful, uplifted, relaxed

TOP MEDICINAL USES
stress, mood enhancement

SIMILAR STRAINS
Sour LA ● p/348
Super Lemon Haze ● p/358
Pineapple ● p/290

Agent Orange is a remarkable resinous bud that produces an amazingly fresh citrus aroma. The high is as uplifting as its aroma and the smooth orange aftertaste makes it a pleasure to smoke. Vaporizing this bud will allow the clean orange flavor to shine through, but hitting this sativa-dominant hybrid from a bong will make for a smooth experience as well—leaving the air and bong water smelling like orange soda. And while the flavor is what will draw you in, the uplifting high is what will keep you coming back.

STRAIN NAME

AK-47 ●

TYPE
hybrid ●

LINEAGE
(Thai × Afghani) × (Colombian ×
Mexican)

SMELL/TASTE
citrus, skunky, sweet

COMMON EFFECTS
euphoria, mellow, cheerful

TOP MEDICINAL USES
pain, mood, enhancement

AWARDS
Cannabis Cup
Highlife Cup

SIMILAR STRAINS
Afghani ● p/56
Skunk #1 ● p/328
MTF ● p/266

AK-47 may sound combative, but this high-quality hybrid is as kind as they come. This world-famous strain is the true definition of a "one-hit wonder," producing a very potent, very long-lasting high after just one toke. The compact buds shine with a pristine coat of crystals and give off a very strong and tart citrus aroma. This strain has been a favorite among growers and smokers for decades and appeals to both sativa and indica lovers with its well-balanced high.

STRAIN NAME

Allen Wrench

TYPE
sativa ●

LINEAGE
Trainwreck × Sour Diesel

SMELL/TASTE
sour, fuel, fruity

COMMON EFFECTS
energetic, creative, alert

TOP MEDICINAL USES
stress, fatigue

SIMILAR STRAINS
NYC Diesel ● p/274
Girl Scout Cookies ● p/182
Champagne ● p/126

By combining the best qualities of two power house parents, Allen Wrench has a room-filling aroma and a head-filling high. The buds' deep and dark green color allows the vivid orange hairs to really pop, creating a nice visual contrast. Its sour fuel aromas dominate the senses with a twist of crisp fruit flavor. The sharp cerebral high is clear, stimulating, and enduring, making Allen Wrench a very dank daytime strain.

STRAIN NAME

Alpha Blue

TYPE
sativa hybrid ●

LINEAGE
Blue Dream × Sour Diesel

SMELL/TASTE
sweet, fruity, musky

COMMON EFFECTS
euphoria, uplifted, energetic

TOP MEDICINAL USES
stress, pain, anxiety

AWARDS
Medical Cannabis Cup

SIMILAR STRAINS
Blue Diesel ● p/92
NYC Diesel ● p/274
Cheese ● p/128

———

The glistening bud of Alpha Blue is like a ball of energy. The immediate euphoria and racing energy felt when smoking this strain produces a clear-functioning high while also providing a body-calming experience— making this a great daytime toke and a highly sought-after medical strain. The aroma is heavily influenced by the Sour Diesel, giving off a sweet, skunky musk, while the complex flavor combinations give it a taste similar to a fruity candy that's been soaked in fuel.

STRAIN NAME

Amnesia Haze ●

TYPE
sativa hybrid ●

LINEAGE
Southeast Asian Sativa × Afghani-Hawaiian

SMELL/TASTE
piney, peppery, fruity

COMMON EFFECTS
energetic, creative, psychedelic

TOP MEDICINAL USES
stress, mood enhancement

AWARDS
Cannabis Cup, Highlife Cup, Spannabis Cup

SIMILAR STRAINS
Super Skunk ● p/364
Trainwreck ● p/372
Super Silver Haze ● p/360

Amnesia Haze is a magnificent hybrid with a world-class genetic makeup. Its old-world flavor is spicy, fruity, and fresh while its effects are soaring. The head high is strong and intense and what you should expect with a name like Amnesia Haze. As with most high-quality haze strains, growing this award-winning strain takes patience, great care, and an expert green thumb—making this an elusive strain to find.

STRAIN NAME

Atomic Northern Lights ●

TYPE
indica hybrid ●

LINEAGE
Northern Lights #5 phenotype

SMELL/TASTE
sweet, skunk, lemon

COMMON EFFECTS
mellow, relaxed, euphoria

TOP MEDICINAL USES
stress, pain

SIMILAR STRAINS
Lemon Skunk ● p/246
Cherry Pie ● p/138
Space Queen ● p/350

———

If you smoke weed, then you've no doubt heard of and most likely smoked a Northern Lights strain—yes, it's that popular. Northern Lights has a worldwide reputation and a history that spans over three decades. Atomic Northern Lights is a Canadian–bred variation of the famed Northern Lights #5. Atomic Northern Lights is endowed with all the same characteristics of its ancestors but said to have a more diverse genetic code, making it a stronger and more robust plant and giving it a more balanced mind–body high.

STRAIN NAME

Berry White ●

TYPE
hybrid ●

LINEAGE
Blueberry × White Widow

SMELL/TASTE
blueberry, sweet, sour

COMMON EFFECTS
energy, body buzz, cheerful

TOP MEDICINAL USES
stress, mood enhancement

SIMILAR STRAINS
Blue Cheese ● p/90
Blueberry Yum Yum ● p/108
Blue Dream ● p/94

This strain is a perfect balance of looks, flavors, and effects. Berry White has a nice blue-tinted color with hints of pine green and orange hairs throughout. The flavor is a complex mix of sweet and sour berry combined with a pleasing earthy and woody finish. The effects of this hybrid reflect its famous parents beautifully, providing an upbeat beginning with a mellow and calming finish. Sometimes going by the name Blue Widow, Berry White is a delicious and satisfying hybrid celebrity.

STRAIN NAME

Big Buddha Cheese ●

TYPE
indica hybrid ●

LINEAGE
Cheese × Afghani

SMELL/TASTE
cheese, skunk, fruity

COMMON EFFECTS
uplifting, relaxed, cheerful

TOP MEDICINAL USES
stress, anxiety

AWARDS
Cannabis Cup

SIMILAR STRAINS
Blue Cheese ● p/90
Head Cheese ● p/206
Skunk #1 ● p/328

Beautiful big, bright, and tight buds with an intense fruity cheese aroma make this Cheese strain variety a stinky delight. Bred specifically to isolate the original British-grown Cheese strain's unique traits, Big Buddha Cheese is considered by Cheese lovers to be an ideal specimen. While the intense cheese flavor overpowers the taste buds, the slow creeping high provides a nice uplifting high without any of the laziness you would expect from such an indica-dominant hybrid.

STRAIN NAME

Bio Diesel

TYPE
hybrid ●

LINEAGE
Sour Diesel × Sensi Star

SMELL/TASTE
fuel, pine, skunk

COMMON EFFECTS
uplifted, cheerful, body buzz

TOP MEDICINAL USES
stress, pain

SIMILAR STRAINS
Sour Diesel ● p/342
Death Star ● p/162
Ogiesel ● p/280

———

Bio Diesel is a powerful strain first bred and grown in Denver, Colorado. This outstanding bud is very stinky, very sticky, and very potent. These nice dense nugs have diesel-dominant characteristics as evident in the pungent aroma and piney aftertaste. The smoke produced from this hard-hitting hybrid will expand your lungs and then quickly expand your mind with its strong sativa presence. The extreme potency of Bio Diesel only requires a few small puffs to provide a long-lasting and well-rounded high.

STRAIN NAME

Black Cherry Soda ●

TYPE
hybrid ●

LINEAGE
unknown (California)

SMELL/TASTE
cherry, creamy, berry

COMMON EFFECTS
relaxed, euphoria, lazy

TOP MEDICINAL USES
stress, pain

SIMILAR STRAINS
Blackberry ● p/86
Fruity Pebbles ● p/174
Bubble Gum ● p/114

The dark, rich purple color of this beautiful strain is what makes this elusive bud a unique treasure. The genetics of the strain are largely unknown but is is thought to have some genetics of the Bubble Gum strain. While the flavor of this bud is a tasty combination of black cherry mixed with a creamy finish (giving it its obvious name), it's the deep and distinct colors that make this strain famous. Its effects are very relaxing and body calming combined with a slight euphoric head rush.

STRAIN NAME

Black Domina ●

TYPE
indica hybrid ●

LINEAGE
(Afghani × Ortega) ×
(Northern Lights × Hash Plant)

SMELL/TASTE
spicy, peppery, musky

COMMON EFFECTS
relaxed, sleepy, body buzz

TOP MEDICINAL USES
insomnia, pain

AWARDS
Spannabis Cup, Highlife Cup

SIMILAR STRAINS
G-13 ● p/176
Blackberry Kush ● p/88
Dead Head OG ● p/160

———————

Reminiscent of some spaced–out autumn foliage, this deep dark green and purple flower might look out of this world but its heavy sedative impact will keep you grounded as it takes over your entire body. While the Hash Plant influence can give its smoke a dense spice and peppery taste, its blend of other elite indicas gives it the stick-to-your-hands resin Black Domina is famous for. This is a great indica that gives a traditional and steady body buzz perfect for an overall body decompression.

STRAIN NAME

Black Tuna ●

TYPE
indica hybrid ●

LINEAGE
Herojuana × Lamb's Bread

SMELL/TASTE
spicy, pungent

COMMON EFFECTS
euphoria, body buzz, couch-lock

TOP MEDICINAL USES
insomnia, muscle tension

SIMILAR STRAINS
Blackberry Kush ● p/88
Lavender ● p/244
MTF ● p/266

Named after a notorious group of marijuana smugglers called the Black Tuna Gang, this powerhouse strain gained instant notoriety throughout Canada for its amazing potency. Heavy couch-lock with a full body buzz makes this knockout strain a heavy-hitting top strain for medical marijuana users.

The leader of the Black Tuna Gang, Robert Platshorn served one of the harshest imprisonments ever for marijuana charges—nearly three decades after being convicted in 1980 for allegedly smuggling over five hundred tons of marijuana from Colombia to Miami between the mid- to late 1970s.

STRAIN NAME
Blackberry

TYPE
hybrid ●

LINEAGE
Black Domina × Raspberry Cough

SMELL/TASTE
fruity, floral, earthy

COMMON EFFECTS
mellow, relaxed, focused

TOP MEDICINAL USES
pain, insomnia, stress

SIMILAR STRAINS
God's Gift ● p/186
Nuken ● p/272
Pre-98 Bubba ● p/300

The tight and dense buds of the Blackberry strain act as a visual precursor to the thick and heavy smoke it will ultimately produce. While the aromas that emanate from the dark-colored nugs are a strong, pungently sweet, and fruity bouquet of odors, the flavor itself is surprisingly subdued. The overall effects are a wide-ranging mix of an indica-induced couch-lock to a sativa-inspired cerebral focus.

STRAIN NAME

Blackberry Kush ●

TYPE
indica hybrid ●

LINEAGE
Blackberry × Afghani

SMELL/TASTE
fuel, berry, spicy

COMMON EFFECTS
relaxed, mellow, euphoria

TOP MEDICINAL USES
pain, appetite

SIMILAR STRAINS
Godfather OG ● p/184
Sugar Daddy ● p/354
Deadhead OG ● p/160

The dense purple and dark green buds of Blackberry Kush are covered in a coating of crystals so heavy they seem to hide the wonderful orange hairs that round out the exotic look of this flower. The brawny buds emit a complex mix of deep fuel and mixed berry aromas and flavors that tingle the nose and please the taste buds. The rich smoke produces a mellow body high without producing a feeling of tiredness or laziness.

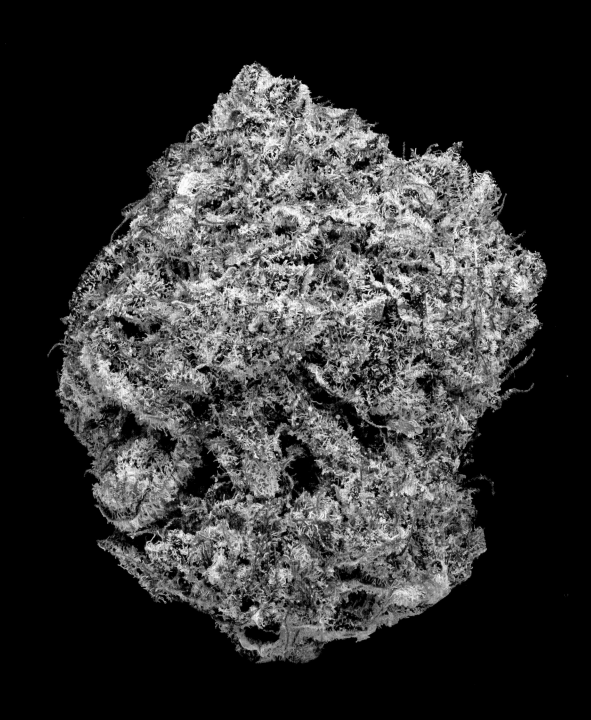

STRAIN NAME

Blue Cheese ●

TYPE
indica hybrid ●

LINEAGE
Blueberry × Big Buddha Cheese

SMELL/TASTE
cheese, creamy, skunky

COMMON EFFECTS
relaxed, calm, uplifting

TOP MEDICINAL USES
stress, muscle tension

AWARDS
Spannabis Cup, Cannabis Cup,
Highlife Cup

SIMILAR STRAINS
Blue Diesel ● p/92
Cheese ● p/128
Chiesel ● p/146

Like its namesake, the bag appeal of this bud might turn some tokers off to this interesting strain. The nugs are a small, average-looking bunch, but what is truly spectacular about Blue Cheese is its astonishing aroma and flavor. The smell and flavor match this strain's name to perfection, a wonderfully pungent mix of fruity blueberry and sharp cheese—making it an absolute joy to smoke. Blue Cheese has common indica characteristics in its high, but it can produce some positive mood enhancements throughout its stoney effects.

STRAIN NAME
Blue Diesel ●

TYPE
hybrid ●

LINEAGE
Blueberry × NYC Diesel

SMELL/TASTE
berry, citrus, piney

COMMON EFFECTS
euphoria, relaxed, cheerful

TOP MEDICINAL USES
pain, stress

SIMILAR STRAINS
Sour Diesel ● p/342
Blue Cheese ● p/90
Blue Dream ● p/94

———

Blue Diesel is another great cross of two famed parents. Unlike most Diesel crosses, the trademark fuel odor that typically dominates the aroma is all but gone—replaced by the sweet, fruity scent of berries. The flavor adds nice piney grapefruit undertones that are undeniably Diesel. The most remarkable trait of this hybrid strain is its perfectly balanced and long-lasting effects that provide a dreamlike head high alongside a satisfying body buzz with no tiredness whatsoever.

STRAIN NAME

Blue Dream ●

TYPE
hybrid ●

LINEAGE
Blueberry × Super Silver Haze

SMELL/TASTE
zesty, sweet, musky

COMMON EFFECTS
creative, alert, uplifted

TOP MEDICINAL USES
stress, mood enhancement

SIMILAR STRAINS
Green Crack ● p/194
Green Ribbon ● p/196
Trainwreck ● p/372

Blue Dream is a popular hybrid with dense popcorn-like buds. Its name is derived not only from its lineage but also from its frosty, trichome-covered buds that shimmer a marvelous blue glow. With one of the best full-bodied flavors of any strain, Blue Dream provides a clear, functioning high that adds instant focus and energy to your system. Thanks in part to its Haze influence, this is a fantastic strain for a wake and bake session, allowing you to accomplish tasks without any laziness or sleepiness.

STRAIN NAME

Blue Hawaiian

TYPE
sativa hybrid ●

LINEAGE
Blueberry × Hawaiian Sativa

SMELL/TASTE
sweet, fruity, tropical

COMMON EFFECTS
energy, cheerful, euphoria

TOP MEDICINAL USES
stress, mood enhancement

SIMILAR STRAINS
Blue Diesel ● p/92
Blueberry Yum Yum ● p/108
Tangie ● p/370

A very sweet and fruity strain, Blue Hawaiian packs a luscious tropical punch. Its light green to orange to pink coloration is a clear expression of its sativa side, while the aroma is a direct influence of the Blueberry. The effects are instantly heady and cerebral, giving off a burst of energy and cheerful happiness. The body eventually catches up to the mind and finishes the high with a nice gradual letdown to relaxation.

STRAIN NAME

Blue Kush ●

TYPE
indica hybrid ●

LINEAGE
Blue Moon Rocks × Sour Bubble

SMELL/TASTE
floral, berry, spicy

COMMON EFFECTS
body buzz, relaxed, alert

TOP MEDICINAL USES
pain, muscle tension

SIMILAR STRAINS
Blue Nightmare ● p/102
GDP ● p/178
Godfather OG ● p/184

———————

Blue Kush is a tasty combination of blueberry and lavender sweetness contrasted with subtle sour and spice undertones. Its heavy indica influence presents itself with a rush of relaxing warmth that is felt immediately throughout your entire body and face—giving this strain its nickname, "Blush." Like its contrasting flavor, the strong body buzz is also agreeably complemented by a nice mental alertness, making the high from Blue Kush more functional and clear.

STRAIN NAME

Blue Moon Rocks ●

TYPE
indica hybrid ●

LINEAGE
Bubble Gum × Blue Moon

SMELL/TASTE
lavender, fruity, tart

COMMON EFFECTS
relaxed, cheerful,

TOP MEDICINAL USES
pain, stress

SIMILAR STRAINS
Sour Bubble ● p/336
Blue Dream ● p/94
Grape Ape ● p/190

Blue Moon Rocks is a very flavorful strain originating from a long line of Blue ancestors. When ground up, the aroma really fills the air with hints of lavender and sweet floral pot-pourri and the extra-smooth smoke amplifies the berry flavor. This indica hybrid has a strong sativa presence, making it a well-rounded workhorse. Blue Moon Rocks will provide a heavier body buzz than most traditional blueberry strains, while adding a peaceful head high that will put you in a tranquil and clearheaded place.

STRAIN NAME

Blue Nightmare ●

TYPE
hybrid ●

LINEAGE
Blueberry × Super Silver Haze

SMELL/TASTE
berry, sweet, floral

COMMON EFFECTS
alert, relaxed, lazy

TOP MEDICINAL USES
muscle tension, appetite

SIMILAR STRAINS
Blue Dream ● p/94
Green Ribbon ● p/196
Green Crack ● p/194

———

Although it has the same parents as the Blue Dream strain, Blue Nightmare's phenotypes lean more toward the Blueberry indica side compared to its popular sativa-dominant sister. The high from Blue Nightmare is still predominately clearheaded but a calming relaxation can be felt through the body, causing a slight laziness in the limbs. And the sweet floral aroma and mouthwatering flavors not only please the palate but also lead to a strong case of the munchies.

STRAIN NAME

Blueberry ●

TYPE
indica hybrid ●

LINEAGE
(Purple Thai × Highland Thai) ×
Afghani

SMELL/TASTE
blueberry, floral, sweet

COMMON EFFECTS
euphoria, mellow, relaxed

TOP MEDICINAL USES
stress, pain

AWARDS
Cannabis Cup

SIMILAR STRAINS
Juicy Fruit ● p/230
Trainwreck ● p/372
Bubble Gum ● p/114

The signature blueberry flavor of this prized strain is matched only by its acclaimed euphoric highs. Created by iconic breeder DJ Short, the bud pictured here is a prime example of this strain—coming directly from the man himself. Coated in purple-blue crystals, Blueberry's potency, aroma, and flavors are renowned as one of the world's finest and make this strain a go-to source when developing and breeding new hybrid crosses.

STRAIN NAME

Blueberry Afgoo ●

TYPE
indica hybrid ●

LINEAGE
Blueberry × Afgoo

SMELL/TASTE
piney, skunky, berry

COMMON EFFECTS
sleepy, couch-lock, body buzz

TOP MEDICINAL USES
insomnia, pain

SIMILAR STRAINS
Burkle ● p/116
Cannatonic ● p/122
God's Gift ● p/186

———

Just looking at the mesmerizing Blueberry Afgoo might be enough to affect your state of mind. This interesting hybrid instantly draws you in with its perfect mix of orange, green, purple, and blue color, which makes it nearly impossible to pick a dominant color to describe this bud. Its indica pedigree is another perfect mix that will send your body into a fully relaxed state and will inevitably drift you off into couch-lock.

STRAIN NAME

Blueberry Yum Yum ●

TYPE
hybrid ●

LINEAGE
unknown (California)

SMELL/TASTE
grape, strawberry, floral

COMMON EFFECTS
sociable, cheerful, euphoria

TOP MEDICINAL USES
mood enhancement, anxiety

SIMILAR STRAINS
Grape Ape ● p/190
Blueberry ● p/104
Cataract ● p/124

The deep, rich blue and purple coloring that spreads across the buds of Blueberry Yum Yum is matched in beauty only by the hefty coating of plump trichome crystals that cover them. And if Blueberry Yum Yum's appearance isn't enough, the fruity, sweet smell and flavor will surely impress the senses. But don't let its pretty exterior and sweet taste fool you; this good-time bud is a powerful one-hit wonder quickly pumping energy and euphoria into one's system with no looking back.

STRAIN NAME

BTY OG●

TYPE
indica ●

LINEAGE
unknown (California)

SMELL/TASTE
piney, sweet, spicy

COMMON EFFECTS
body buzz, relaxed, couch-lock

TOP MEDICINAL USES
pain, appetite

SIMILAR STRAINS
True OG ● p/376
Cataract ● p/124
XXX OG ● p/390

———

This dank Kush is quite literally "better than your" OG. This heavily frosted flower is one of the most potent OG strains with its off-the-chart THC levels. The nugs are visually more voluminous than your typical OG but are nonetheless superdense, supersticky, and humming with pungent odors. All the expected indica traits are in full effect with an intense and long-lasting full-body melt that is deep and unyielding.

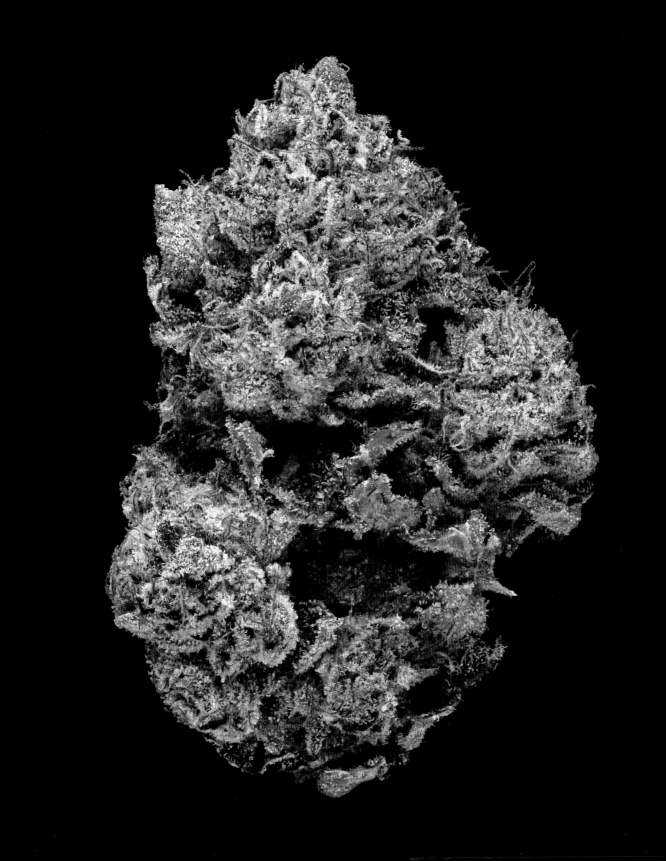

STRAIN NAME
Bubba Kush ⬤

TYPE
indica hybrid ⬤

LINEAGE
Bubble Gum × OG Kush

SMELL/TASTE
musky, sweet, earthy

COMMON EFFECTS
relaxing, couch-lock, sleepy

TOP MEDICINAL USES
pain, insomnia

SIMILAR STRAINS
Master Kush ⬤ p/256
Burkle ⬤ p/116
GDP ⬤ p/178

————

Bubba Kush is known for producing an intense body-numbing stone and its long-lasting narcotic effects are highly sought after in the medical marijuana community. The sweetness of Bubble Gum really cuts through the sour pine Kush flavors, making for a nice diverse flavor profile. The heavy, thick smoke is a precursor to the heavy couch-lock effect that makes this robust indica a true knockout.

STRAIN NAME

Bubble Gum

TYPE
hybrid

LINEAGE
unknown (Indiana)

SMELL/TASTE
sweet, candy, fruity

COMMON EFFECTS
uplifting, euphoria, inspiring

TOP MEDICINAL USES
anxiety, mood enhancement

AWARDS
Cannabis Cup, Spannabis Cup

SIMILAR STRAINS
Cotton Candy ● p/152
Blueberry ● p/104
Juicy Fruit ● p/230

The nose knows, and once you smell this extraordinary bud you will realize why it's aptly named Bubble Gum. With a nice split between head and body highs, Bubble Gum is a true hybrid strain that comes from a storied and unstable past. Originally grown in the state of Indiana in the 1970s, it wasn't until recently that growers in Amsterdam attempted to stabilize and clone this strain for growing consistent crops. And they finally did. And it's delicious.

STRAIN NAME

Burkle ●

TYPE
indica hybrid ●

LINEAGE
Bubba Kush × Urkle

SMELL/TASTE
sweet, berry, sour

COMMON EFFECTS
calm, lazy, relaxed

TOP MEDICINAL USES
insomnia, pain

SIMILAR STRAINS
GDP ● p/178
Grape Ape ● p/190
Querkle ● p/314

Burkle is an amazingly colorful and remarkably intense-looking bud even when you're not high. Its pallet of greens, purples, oranges, and crystal blues all seem to meld into one surreal and awesome nugget just begging to be smoked. And when you do, be prepared for a steady and soothing body euphoria that will calm your entire anatomy. Sit back and relax because you won't want to—or physically be able to—do much more than just chill with the Burkle.

STRAIN NAME

Candy Chem

TYPE
sativa hybrid ●

LINEAGE
Chemdawg × Snowdog

SMELL/TASTE
sweet, acrid, earthy

COMMON EFFECTS
uplifting, euphoria, creative

TOP MEDICINAL USES
fatigue, mood enhancement

SIMILAR STRAINS
Cheese ● p/128
Snocap ● p/332
NYC Diesel ● p/274

This Chemdawg variety grows in a nice pointy bud shape that appears almost white with trichomes. The complex aroma of sweet earth is amplified as you break it apart. The flavor adds the very crisp and acidic taste you would expect from a Chemdawg offspring. Very euphoric from the get go, Candy Chem hits with a rush of uplifting energy that evens out into an inspiring and clear state of mind.

STRAIN NAME

Cannalope Haze ●

TYPE
sativa ●

LINEAGE
Haze × Mexican Michoacán Sativa

SMELL/TASTE
melon, sweet, tropical

COMMON EFFECTS
cheerful, uplifted, creative

TOP MEDICINAL USES
stress, nausea

SIMILAR STRAINS
Chocolope ● p/144
Chocolate Thunder ● p/142
Tangie ● p/370

Breeders love Cannalope Haze for its quick flowering time and consistently good yields, but this strain is definitely renowned for its distinct melon taste. Cannalope Haze's sweet aromas transition perfectly into the intense, sultry flavors that linger on your tongue well after enjoying this smooth smoke. A delectable treat especially when smoked through a vaporizer or water pipe, these resinous buds will provide a very heady high that can be felt in both your temples and eyes.

STRAIN NAME

Cannatonic ●

TYPE
hybrid ●

LINEAGE
MK-Ultra × G-13

SMELL/TASTE
lemony, piney, earthy

COMMON EFFECTS
body buzz, alert, couch-lock

TOP MEDICINAL USES
pain, muscle tension

AWARDS
Medical Cannabis Cup
Cannabis Cup

SIMILAR STRAIN
Harlequin ● p/198

Cannatonic is a very interesting hybrid. It grows like a traditional indica, smells like a typical sativa, and has a unique nearly 1:1 ratio of THC to CBD. This medical marijuana wonder is a very dense flower with sticky honey-like crystals that give it a wonderful golden glow. The flavor and aroma are subtle, but the effects are what make Cannatonic so special. The "catatonic" body high creeps in slowly but eventually takes hold and it's as heavy and relaxing as they come. The low THC ratio leaves your head completely clear, keeping all the focus entirely on the body.

STRAIN NAME

Cataract ●

TYPE
indica ●

LINEAGE
LA Confidential × OG Kush

SMELL/TASTE
citrus, fuel, fruity

COMMON EFFECTS
body buzz, euphoria, couch-lock

TOP MEDICINAL USES
pain, appetite, insomnia

AWARDS
Medical Cannabis Cup

SIMILAR STRAINS
BTY OG ● p/110
Triangle ● p/374
Girl Scout Cookies ● p/182

The superdense buds of Cataract have a very unique color palette that shimmer in a heroic silver tinge. The flavors are very characteristic of a Kush with an indica high that is exceptionally strong. This fortified strain is definitely a nighttime toke that shouldn't be taken for granted. The high is a serious creeper that will continue to slowly build and intensify long after the last hit—so puff cautiously.

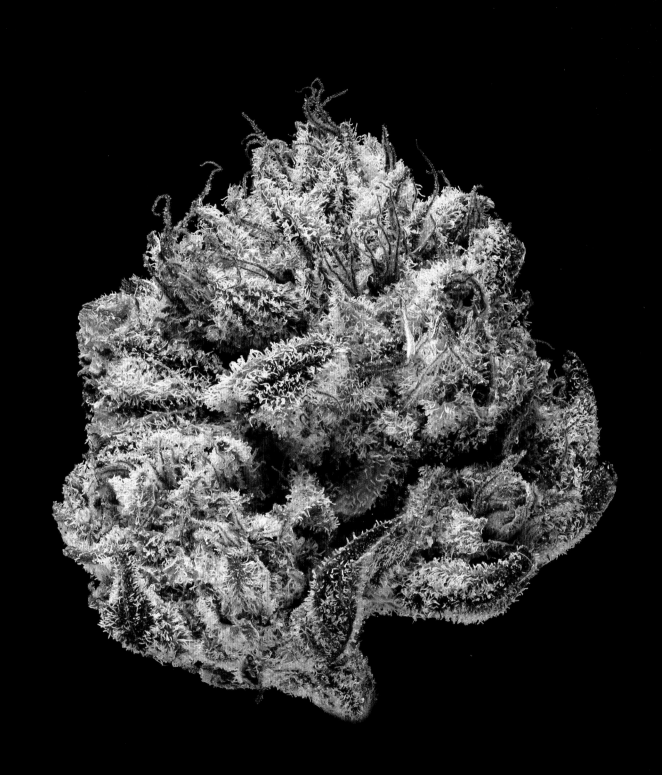

STRAIN NAME

Champagne

TYPE
hybrid ●

LINEAGE
Hash Plant × unknown (OG Kush phenotype)

SMELL/TASTE
floral, sweet, citrus

COMMON EFFECTS
cheerful, relaxed, sociable

TOP MEDICINAL USES
appetite, muscle tension

SIMILAR STRAINS
AK-47 ● p/64
Juicy Fruit ● p/230
Allen Wrench ● p/66

This bubbly, sweet strain may not be an actual sparkling wine but its buds absolutely sparkle with pristine trichome crystals. The aromas are subtle and sweet with a soft hash flavor to finish. Just like its namesake, the smoke will go straight to your head with a nice even energy and a perfect body buzz that lingers. This long-lasting high makes Champagne a great strain for get-togethers and social activities.

STRAIN NAME

Cheese ●

TYPE
hybrid ●

LINEAGE
Skunk #1 × Afghani

SMELL/TASTE
cheese, skunk, spicy

COMMON EFFECTS
body buzz, relaxed, uplifted

TOP MEDICINAL USES
pain, appetite

AWARDS
Cannabis Cup, Emerald Cup,
Spannabis Cup,

SIMILAR STRAINS
Big Buddha Cheese ● p/76
Head Cheese ● p/206
Headband ● p/208

Cheese, also known as U.K. Cheese, originated in the United Kingdom in the late 1980s
and has ever since been one of the most
popular strains for crossbreeding other
cheesy varieties. Big beautiful buds and a
musky cheesy smell are the calling card of this
important strain that provides both a soothing body stone and a focused energy—
making Cheese a high-quality hybrid that
pleases the mind, body, and taste buds.

STRAIN NAME

Chemband ●

TYPE
sativa hybrid ●

LINEAGE
Chemdawg × Headband

SMELL/TASTE
earthy, metallic, fuel

COMMON EFFECTS
energetic, euphoria, cheerful

TOP MEDICINAL USES
fatigue, appetite

SIMILAR STRAINS
Sour Diesel ● p/342
Girl Scout Cookies ● p/182
NYC Diesel ● p/274

Chemband crosses two favorite sativas to produce a dense, diesel-like flower that absolutely reeks of pungent fuel. The thick smoke produces a much more "chemmy" and bitter flavor that hits heavy. Just like the Headband strain, Chemband affects the head with an instant surge of energy that tickles your forehead and eyes. This is a great daytime strain that will get your heart racing and your body moving.

STRAIN NAME

Chemdawg

TYPE
sativa hybrid ●

LINEAGE
unknown

SMELL/TASTE
sour, lemon, pine, spicy

COMMON EFFECTS
uplifting, creative, euphoria

TOP MEDICINAL USES
pain, appetite, stress

AWARDS
Emerald Cup, Medical Cannabis Cup

SIMILAR STRAINS
Sour Diesel ● p/342
Super Lemon Haze ● p/358
Holy Grail ● p/214

Shrouded in a genetic mystery, Chemdawg is perhaps one of the most influential strains today due in part to its tangy fuel odor that has since become a hallmark of so many fine strains. Chemdawg is also responsible for spawning some of the most sought-after strains, including East and West Coast rivals Sour Diesel and OG Kush. Chemdawg is not just superstinky but this trichome-rich bud is supersticky and potent. Just one hit from this legendary bud will make you understand why this strain is so idolized.

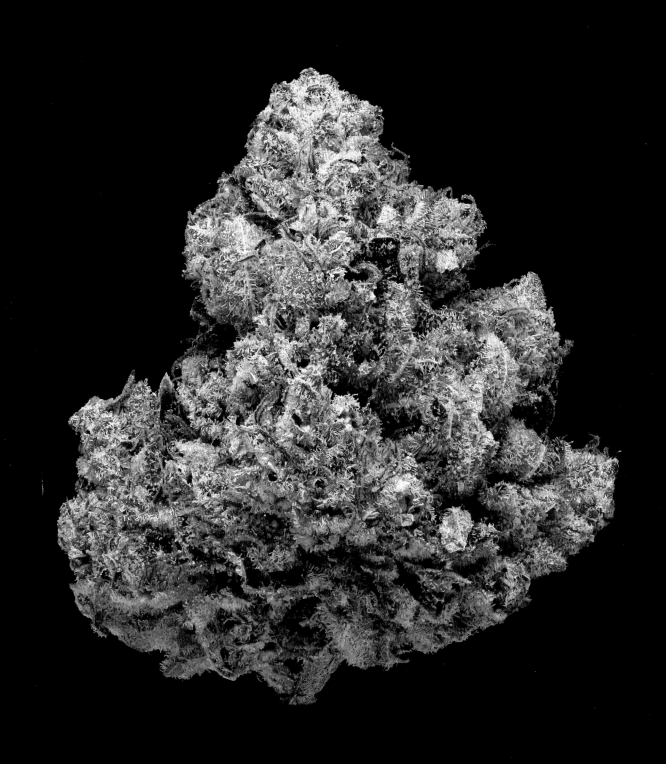

STRAIN NAME

Chernobyl

TYPE
sativa hybrid ●

LINEAGE
(Trainwreck × Trinity) × Jack the Ripper

SMELL/TASTE
vanilla, lemon, creamy

COMMON EFFECTS
body buzz, relaxed, euphoria

TOP MEDICINAL USES
muscle tension, stress

SIMILAR STRAINS
Jack Herer ● p/222
Super Lemon Haze ● p/358
Jack Skellington ● p/226

With irresistible old-school looks and a truly unique aroma, Chernobyl is far from a nuclear disaster. Named for its devastating potency and flavor, this experimental hybrid has a pronounced flavor that can only be described as lemon-sherbet. While the smooth palate-clearing smoke is a taste sensation, Chernobyl also creates a very long-lasting cerebral high that is unexpectedly accompanied by a full body–buzz fallout.

STRAIN NAME

Cherry AK

TYPE
sativa hybrid ●

LINEAGE
AK-47 phenotype

SMELL/TASTE
skunky, cherry, acrid

COMMON EFFECTS
uplifted, energetic, spacey

TOP MEDICINAL USES
fatigue, nausea

SIMILAR STRAINS
Tangie ● p/370
Afwreck ● p/60
Skunk #1 ● p/328

Cherry AK, often referred to simply as Cherry, is a legendary pheno of the renowned AK-47 strain. These soft buds are infused with luscious red hairs that only begin to entice you with their cherry attraction. The signature skunky flavor that AK-47 is known for is amplified with the singular and profound taste of bold cherry candies. If the spectacular taste isn't enough, the cerebral rush is a fast-acting, high-octane, and all-out uplifting mental high that makes for an ideal wake and bake session.

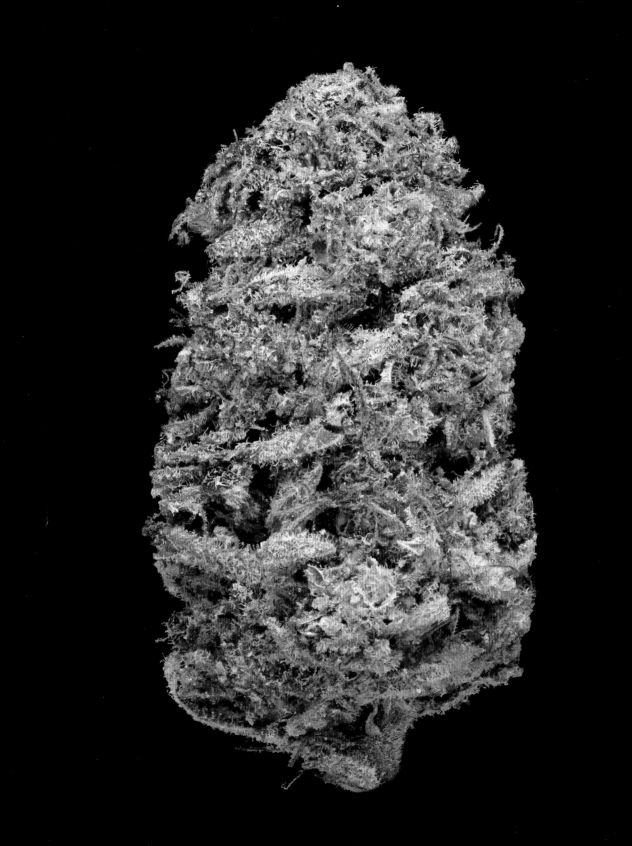

STRAIN NAME

Cherry Pie

TYPE
hybrid

LINEAGE
GDP × Durban Poison

SMELL/TASTE
lemon, cherry, acrid

COMMON EFFECTS
body buzz, relaxing, focused

TOP MEDICINAL USES
stress, anxiety

AWARD
Cannabis Cup

SIMILAR STRAINS
Girl Scout Cookies p/182
Grape Ape p/190
White Widow p/386

Cherry Pie literally reeks of sweet and sour cherries. The dark dense buds of this cherry bomb are beautifully saturated in a thick, clear amber resin that is infused throughout the entire flower. The flavor hits with an acrid spice that smokes fast to produce a high that's instantly uplifting coupled with a long-lasting body buzz devoid of any laziness or fatigue.

STRAIN NAME

Cherry Pie Kush

TYPE
sativa hybrid ●

LINEAGE
(OG Kush × Urkle) × Durban Poison

SMELL/TASTE
sweet, cherry, peppery

COMMON EFFECTS
energetic, cheerful, alert

TOP MEDICINAL USES
appetite, mood enhancement

SIMILAR STRAINS
Afwreck ● p/60
Berry White ● p/74
Vanilla Haze ● p/380

Cherry Pie Kush is a flawless mash-up of three powerhouse parents. The bud itself visually portrays the three distinct parents, twisting and fusing together into a perfect mix of colorful hues, stacked textures, and impressive resin production. The flavors and aromas are a complex medley of sweet cherries, peppery grapes, and sour lemons that produce a smooth and creamy smoke. The effects don't waste any time affecting the mind and body with a happy and joyful sensation that continues to creep throughout the high.

STRAIN NAME

Chocolate Thunder ●

TYPE
sativa hybrid ●

LINEAGE
Chocolope × MTF

SMELL/TASTE
cocoa, creamy, fruity

COMMON EFFECTS
euphoria, cheerful, focused

TOP MEDICINAL USES
anxiety, fatigue

SIMILAR STRAINS
Cannalope Haze ● p/120
Vanilla Haze ● p/380
Island Sweet Skunk ● p/218

With its wispy fiery hairs and bright green color, Chocolate Thunder may not look as powerful as it sounds but one puff and you'll be certain why it's been appropriately named. By combining two chocolaty parents, Chocolate Thunder produces a rich, creamy, and unrivaled chocolate-flavored smoke that is as divine as the energetic high it produces.

STRAIN NAME

Chocolope

TYPE
sativa hybrid ●

LINEAGE
Chocolate Thai × Cannalope Haze

SMELL/TASTE
creamy, fruity, cocoa

COMMON EFFECTS
focused, alert, energetic

TOP MEDICINAL USES
mood enhancement, fatigue

AWARDS
Cannabis Cup, Highlife Cup,
Spannabis Cup

SIMILAR STRAINS
Black Domina ● p/82
Island Sweet Skunk ● p/218
Chocolate Thunder ● p/142

This extremely sweet and flavorful smoke has a brilliant cocoa finish (think cantaloupe melon infused with a touch of chocolate), making this one of the tastiest treats you can get your hands on. But don't let its sweetness fool you. This sativa dominated hybrid is a new-school offspring of some powerful hazey parents. The immediate mental shift you will experience when enjoying this strain will keep you energized, positive, and focused throughout your day. Newbies to this strain should tread lightly though, as its impact could be overwhelming.

STRAIN NAME

Chiesel ●

TYPE
sativa hybrid ●

LINEAGE
Big Buddha Cheese × NYC Diesel

SMELL/TASTE
cheese, fuel, spicy

COMMON EFFECTS
creative, cheerful, body buzz

TOP MEDICINAL USES
stress, anxiety

SIMILAR STRAINS
Head Cheese ● p/206
Cheese ● p/128
Sour Diesel ● p/342

———

This modern-breeding masterpiece provides a funky flavor combination that is as unique as it is delicious. Chiesel is a unification of two very intense and very familiar cannabis aromas—cheese and diesel fuel. Chiesel borders on the sativa-dominant side with its long fluffy buds, while the effects are a pleasing mix of cerebral enlightenment and a mellow body stone.

STRAIN NAME

Cinderella 99

TYPE
sativa hybrid ●

LINEAGE
Jack Herer × Shiva Skunk

SMELL/TASTE
pineapple, tropical, skunky

COMMON EFFECTS
energetic, euphoria, cheerful

TOP MEDICINAL USES
mood enhancement, anxiety

SIMILAR STRAINS
J1 ● p/220
Blueberry ● p/104
Juicy Fruit ● p/230

Also known as C 99 or Cindy for short, Cinderella 99 is a premium slow-smoking bud. It's a nice sativa-dominant hybrid with dense buds and delicious flavor. The aroma is very subtle, but once broken up the tropical skunkiness really come out. Its smooth smoke produces a pineapple flavor that hits fast, resulting in bursts of energy and fits of laughter. Cinderella 99 is an upper-class sativa worthy of being a princess.

STRAIN NAME

Congolese Sativa

TYPE
sativa

LINEAGE
Landrace (Africa)

SMELL/TASTE
nutty, earthy, spicy

COMMON EFFECTS
energetic, focused, euphoria

TOP MEDICINAL USES
nausea, stress

SIMILAR STRAINS
Trainwreck p/372
Red Congo p/316
Old Mendo Haze p/284

This African landrace is a colorful strain that comes from one of the continent's largest countries. After countless years of adapting to its environment, Congolese is a colorful and complex sativa with a wonderful nutty and spicy flavor profile. Its effects provide a floating euphoria that is clear, focused, and full of long-lasting energy.

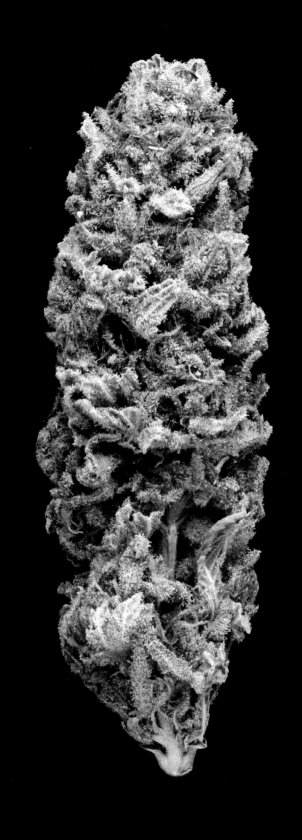

STRAIN NAME

Cotton Candy ●

TYPE
indica hybrid ●

LINEAGE
Lavender × Power Plant

SMELL/TASTE
sweet, piney, floral

COMMON EFFECTS
mellow, body buzz, relaxed

TOP MEDICINAL USES
pain, appetite

AWARD
Emerald Cup

SIMILAR STRAINS
Bubble Gum ● p/114
GDP ● p/178
Grape Ape ● p/190

Perfectly named, this frosty strain is so tasty that it will remind you exactly of the cotton candy from your local carnival. This sweet rarity may seem like a novelty, but this is a complex strain with a genetic lineage that cannabis connoisseurs dream about. Its unique blend of diverse skunk heritage matched with the subtle sativa of the Power Plant gives this visual tour de force an uncanny ability to soothe the body without any drowsiness.

STRAIN NAME

Crack Kush ●

TYPE
indica hybrid ●

LINEAGE
Green Crack × OG Kush

SMELL/TASTE
candy, fruity, earthy

COMMON EFFECTS
euphoria, relaxed, body buzz

TOP MEDICINAL USES
pain, insomnia

SIMILAR STRAINS
XXX OG ● p/390
Louis XIII ● p/248
True OG ● p/376

Crack Kush is a superpotent, high-grade indica hybrid made famous in California's medical marijuana dispensaries. It hits like a brick with a full-body euphoria that eventually transitions into a relaxing body meltdown. Crack Kush often goes by the name "Charlie Sheen," renamed after the infamous actor had a public "meltdown" of his own.

STRAIN NAME

Crystal Coma ●

TYPE
hybrid ●

LINEAGE
unknown (California)

SMELL/TASTE
cheese, musky, earthy

COMMON EFFECTS
relaxed, spacey, sleepy

TOP MEDICINAL USES
insomnia, stress

AWARDS
Medical Cannabis Cup

SIMILAR STRAINS
Chiesel ● p/146
Sour Diesel ● p/342
Head Cheese ● p/206

With THC levels surpassing 26%, it's no wonder Crystal Coma is well known as a top-shelf medical strain. A nighttime only smoke, these buds are stacked with crystals and the flavors are noticeably skunky and absolutely intoxicating. The deep, relaxing stone is very crippling, draining all your energy and instilling a heavy trance-like state over your entire mind and body. Crystal Coma is a definite knockout strain.

STRAIN NAME

Daywrecker ●

TYPE
hybrid ●

LINEAGE
Headband × NYC Diesel

SMELL/TASTE
piney, fuel, lemon

COMMON EFFECTS
euphoria, cheerful, mellow

TOP MEDICINAL USES
anxiety, stress

SIMILAR STRAINS
Sour Diesel ● p/342
Chemdawg ● p/132
Crystal Coma ● p/156

The name may sound cynical, but the fast-acting high that Daywrecker produces is as positive as they come. It was only a matter of time before Headband and NYC Diesel were crossbred and the result is better than expected: a fuel-filled resin bomb that will have you flying high but without racing energy. The mellow euphoria will consume your entire mind and body, leaving you with nothing else to do but enjoy the ride.

STRAIN NAME

Dead Head OG ●

TYPE
hybrid ●

LINEAGE
Chemdawg × SFV OG

SMELL/TASTE
lemon, fuel, earthy

COMMON EFFECTS
euphoria, cheerful, body buzz

TOP MEDICINAL USES
stress, mood enhancement

AWARDS
Cannabis Cup

SIMILAR STRAINS
Holy Grail ● p/214
Bio Diesel ● p/78
Blackberry Kush ● p/88

Dead Head OG is one of the most sticky and pleasantly stinky Kush strains around. This bud is absolutely covered in frosty trichomes, making it hard to appreciate the wonderful purple and green hues that mix into a glorious gradient of color. Once you break apart this resinous nug, the fierce lemon fuel scent will rip through the air and consume the entire room. The buzz that follows is a deep head-to-toe buzz that lifts your spirits and continues its steady high for hours on end.

STRAIN NAME

Death Star

TYPE
hybrid

LINEAGE
Sour Diesel × Sensi Star

SMELL/TASTE
fuel, skunk, citrus

COMMON EFFECTS
euphoria, uplifted, relaxed

TOP MEDICINAL USES
pain, stress, anxiety

AWARD
Medical Cannabis Cup
Cannabis Cup

SIMILAR STRAINS
Chemdawg p/132
NYC Diesel p/274
Sour LA p/348

This classic-looking strain has great jar appeal with its saturated dark green body, vibrant orange-to-brown hairs, and a bright covering of stacked trichomes. Its parents are two of the most acclaimed strains in their own right, although Death Star's smell and flavor favor its Diesel side. Combine this with its powerful potency and you're left with a strain that lives up to its galactic namesake. Death Star may be a one-hit quitter for some but for those with a better tolerance, it will have you riding a fun roller coaster of soaring highs and body-relaxing lows.

STRAIN NAME

Dirty Hairy

TYPE
hybrid ●

LINEAGE
Grapefruit × Herijuana

SMELL/TASTE
fruity, grapefruit, earthy

COMMON EFFECTS
body buzz, euphoria, mellow

TOP MEDICINAL USES
muscle tension, stress

SIMILAR STRAINS
Sweet Tooth ● p/366
Strawberry Cough ● p/352
P91 ● p/286

It's safe to say Dirty Hairy gets its name from the superlong and yarn-like hairs that protrude from this bright green bud. This messy-looking flower has a crisp and clean grapefruit flavor with a musky and earthy finish that's a delight to smoke. The effects hit hard like a body shot straight from Dirty Harry himself, creating a mellow body buzz that's as relaxing as it is euphoric.

STRAIN NAME

Durban Poison

TYPE
sativa●

LINEAGE
Landrace (South Africa)

SMELL/TASTE
sweet, licorice, mint, fruity

COMMON EFFECTS
euphoria, uplifting, creative

TOP MEDICINAL USES
stress, anxiety, pain

AWARDS
Medical Cannabis Cup
Cannabis Cup

SIMILAR STRAINS
Congolese Sativa ● p/150
King's Bread ● p/232
Red Congo ● p/316

Durban Poison is named after the South African port city of Durban, where it originated nearly 50 years ago. This wild-natured sativa is still one of the best pure sativas still being grown today and for good reason. DP is a serious sativa that will instantly have your head sky-high while leaving your body behind with no body fatigue—making this a perfect daytime toke. The Poison's deep colors and sticky, tight appearance coupled with its stimulating long-lasting cerebral effects give this legendary strain a distinct quality that lives up to its hype.

STRAIN NAME

Dutch Treat ●

TYPE
hybrid ●

LINEAGE
unknown (Amsterdam)

SMELL/TASTE
citrus, minty, oily

COMMON EFFECTS
relaxing, euphoria, uplifting

TOP MEDICINAL USES
stress, muscle tension

SIMILAR STRAINS
Lamb's Bread ● p/240
XJ-13 ● p/388
Jack Herer ● p/222

The golden trichome covering on this popular Amsterdam strain is the signature feature that makes this bud a standout hybrid. These flavorful trichomes contain a sweet mix of citrus and pine oil tastes with a clean, minty finish. The immediate uplifting burst will steadily slow down into a relaxing stone that is steady and blissful.

The public sale and consumption of cannabis is allowed within hundreds of licensed "coffee shops" throughout the Netherlands. This decriminalized status has been in effect since 1976 and has since made Amsterdam a hotbed for some of the greatest cannabis seed producers in the world.

STRAIN NAME

Euphoria ●

TYPE
sativa hybrid ●

LINEAGE
unknown (Skunk genetics)

SMELL/TASTE
floral, woody, sweet

COMMON EFFECTS
euphoria, uplifted, sociable

TOP MEDICINAL USES
stress, anxiety

AWARDS
Cannabis Cup, Highlife Cup

SIMILAR STRAINS
Cataract ● p/124
Blueberry Afgoo ● p/106
Purple Dawg ● p/308

Euphoria can be both a physical and mental state and this strain achieves both. The physical euphoria comes from the plant's ability to grow strong and healthy with minimal effort or hassle. And while Euphoria may be a strong flower, the aromas are a gentle perfume of sweet blossoms. The mental state of euphoria comes into play immediately after smoking and promotes an uplifting energy that will have you feeling blissful.

STRAIN NAME

Fire OG ●

TYPE
hybrid ●

LINEAGE
OG Kush phenotype

SMELL/TASTE
lemon, acrid, piney

COMMON EFFECTS
sleepy, relaxing, euphoria

TOP MEDICINAL USES
muscle tension, insomnia

SIMILAR STRAINS
SFV OG ● p/324
Skywalker ● p/330
True OG ● p/376

Fire OG is known for being an all-around powerhouse strain for its strength and flavor. The superdense and stacked buds of Fire OG twinkle with vivid red–orange hairs that seem to light up this dank Kush pheno. The lemon and pine aromas hit the nose as soon as the jar is opened, and the pine cleaner flavors expand the lungs with just a small hit. The effects begin with a balanced head-and-body high, transitioning to mostly body—putting it in a very serene place.

STRAIN NAME

Fruity Pebbles ●

TYPE
hybrid ●

LINEAGE
unknown (California)

SMELL/TASTE
sweet, fruity, creamy

COMMON EFFECTS
cheerful, uplifted, body buzz

TOP MEDICINAL USES
stress, mood enhancement

SIMILAR STRAINS
Grape Ape ● p/190
Grape Romulan ● p/192
Juicy Fruit ● p/230

This strain gives new meaning to a bowl full of Fruity Pebbles. Tasting similar to the cereal with a similar name, Fruity Pebbles is a sweet treat. This frosty flower has a subtle aroma but makes up for it with it fruity and creamy flavor. The expansive smoke can be a bit harsh to some, so sipping from a vaporizer is the best way to appreciate this nug. The effects take a bit to come on, but when they take affect they produce a nice and balanced hybrid high.

STRAIN NAME

G-13 ●

TYPE
indica ●

LINEAGE
unknown (Mississippi)

SMELL/TASTE
earthy, musky, woody

COMMON EFFECTS
euphoria, cheerful, relaxed

TOP MEDICINAL USES
appetite, stress

SIMILAR STRAINS
Afghani ● p/56
AK-47 ● p/64
Mr. Nice Guy ● p/264

G-13 is a legendary strain that is rumored to have been born and bred by the U.S. government in the 1970s. Although a series of twenty-three clones were thought to have been cultivated at the University of Mississippi, only plant number thirteen somehow escaped and the rest is history. This urban legend has since become a go-to choice when creating many of today's popular hybrid crosses. This rare daytime indica has a very unique ability to provide an uplifting full-body high with no tiredness and a clear mind. G-13 is a superspecimen of a pure indica.

The University of Mississippi is home to the only U.S. government–sanctioned cannabis farm and lab. They have been growing, storing, documenting, and studying cannabis since 1968—all paid for by U.S. taxpayers.

STRAIN NAME

GDP ●

(Granddaddy Purple)

TYPE
indica ●

LINEAGE
Big Bud × Urkle

SMELL/TASTE
grape, creamy, berry

COMMON EFFECTS
euphoria, relaxed, body buzz

TOP MEDICINAL USES
pain, appetite

AWARD
Cannabis Cup

SIMILAR STRAINS
Grape Ape ● p/190
Purple Sticky Punch ● p/312
Lavender ● p/244

———

Deep purples and a glossy crystal coat make GDP an absolutely gorgeous bud, but Granddaddy Purple's looks are just as intense as its traits. The distinct flavors and aromas of GDP are an unforgettable combination of creamy grape berries that make for a smooth smoke session each time. But despite its celebrated looks and aromas, GDP is perhaps best known for its deep, full-body melt and considered one of the best indica strains in the medical marijuana community.

STRAIN NAME

Ghost ●

TYPE
hybrid ●

LINEAGE
OG Kush phenotype

SMELL/TASTE
pine, citrus, astringent

COMMON EFFECTS
cheerful, uplifted, sociable

TOP MEDICINAL USES
mood enhancement, anxiety

AWARDS
Medical Cannabis Cup

SIMILAR STRAINS
Triangle ● p/374
SFV OG ● p/324
Holy Grail ● p/214

Thought by some to be the "original" OG Kush or possibly just a direct pheno of its sister strain known as Triangle, the one thing that's for certain is that Ghost is clearly on the sativa side of OG Kush hybrids. Ghost's kushy flavors and aromas—citrus, spicy pine, and lemon cleaner—are the cleanest and clearest of all the OG varieties. And the cerebral high is just as clear as the flavors, delivering a happy and positive effect that is strong but not overpowering, making for a nice social and functioning high.

STRAIN NAME

Girl Scout Cookies ●

Type
hybrid ●

LINEAGE
Triangle × F1 Durban

SMELL/TASTE
fruity, spicy, fuel

COMMON EFFECTS
euphoria, uplifting, relaxed

TOP MEDICINAL USES
anxiety, stress, pain,

AWARDS
Cannabis Cup, Medical Cannabis Cup

SIMILAR STRAINS
Berry White ● p/74
Cotton Candy ● p/152
Cherry Pie ● p/138

With the pedigree of two legendary strains, it is no wonder Girl Scout Cookies has created a worldwide buzz. This modern-day San Francisco treat is the perfect balance of these parental all-stars—the buds are fluffy and dense, the flavor is a fuel-filled spicy mint, and the effects are both mind-numbing and body melting. Its mouthwatering appearance, fresh one-of-a-kind "Thin Mints" flavor, and enduring spacey high make this bud a triple threat for any connoisseur. This premier strain is an all-around stunner and one of the most versatile strains—appealing to both indica and sativa lovers alike.

Renamed in 1847, San Francisco was originally called Yerba Buena, which translates to "good herb."

STRAIN NAME
Godfather OG ●

TYPE
indica hybrid ●

LINEAGE
GDP × OG Kush

SMELL/TASTE
spicy, skunky, grape

COMMON EFFECTS
euphoric, relaxed, mellow

TOP MEDICINAL USES
appetite, insomnia

AWARDS
Medical Cannabis Cup

SIMILAR STRAINS
Abusive OG ● p/54
XXX OG ● p/390
Louis XIII ● p/248

The don of OGs, Godfather OG takes the old-school flavor of OG Kush and combines it with the grape and berry tartness of GDP, resulting in a complex and savory smoke. Godfather OG boasts some of the highest THC percentages in the medical marijuana scene, making this strain a very potent medicine known for giving a deep and intense full-body relaxation accompanied by a serious case of the munchies.

STRAIN NAME

God's Gift ●

TYPE
indica hybrid ●

LINEAGE
(Cinderella 99 × G-13) × Urkle

SMELL/TASTE
grape, citrus, creamy

COMMON EFFECTS
sleepy, lazy, relaxed

TOP MEDICINAL USES
insomnia, pain, appetite

SIMILAR STRAINS
GDP ● p/178
Grape Ape ● p/190
Cotton Candy ● p/152

God's "gift" can be seen in both the sumptuous appearance and the superstrong, consistent potency this strain is blessed with. A hard-hitting bud from the California dispensary scene, God's Gift puts your body into a deep, heavy, trance-like state that continues to creep throughout the entire body high. The fresh and flavorful smoke this majestic bud produces not only whets your whistle but also whets your appetite thanks to its unusually high THC content—so get comfortable and beware of the munchies.

STRAIN NAME

Goo Berry ●

TYPE
indica hybrid ●

LINEAGE
Afgoo × Blueberry

SMELL/TASTE
berry, piney, oily

COMMON EFFECTS
sleepy, body buzz, cheerful

TOP MEDICINAL USES
pain, insomnia

SIMILAR STRAINS
Northern Blueberry ● p/268
Romulan Berry ● p/322
Burkle ● p/116

Goo Berry not only looks like but also actually tastes just like a resinous Christmas tree. With some additional hints of sweet berry, this greasy bud is a heavy hitter with strong indica effects. She'll bring out your jolly spirit while soothing your senses with a strong tingle that can be felt up through your head and out to your toes, making for a perfect nightcap.

STRAIN NAME

Grape Ape ⬤

TYPE
indica hybrid ⬤

LINEAGE
Afghani × Skunk #1

SMELL/TASTE
fruity, sour, earthy

COMMON EFFECTS
mellow, lazy, sleepy

TOP MEDICINAL USES
pain, appetite

SIMILAR STRAINS
GDP ⬤ p/178
Bubble Gum ⬤ p/114
Purple Sticky Punch ⬤ p/312

———

Grape Ape is a star among the purple strains. Its dense nugs boast an ultrafruity bouquet and the flavor is on point with a grape bubble gum or Kool-Aid. This delicious strain is sure to please any nose and palate. Its looks can vary slightly depending on the phenotype—from a green-purple to all-over purple—and can easily be confused for the Granddaddy Purple (GDP) strain. Although it may not be as crystal-coated as GDP, it no doubt offers a strong, tranquil stone while leaving your head fog free and clear.

STRAIN NAME

Grape Romulan ●

TYPE
hybrid ●

LINEAGE
Romulan × Grapefruit

SMELL/TASTE
sweet, floral, metallic

COMMON EFFECTS
focused, uplifted, body buzz

TOP MEDICINAL USES
anxiety, pain

SIMILAR STRAINS
Sour Grape ● p/346
Cotton Candy ● p/152
Fruity Pebbles ● p/174

Grape Romulan joins two powerful Canadian superstars into one compelling hybrid. Its shiny amber resins give this superdense bud a light and frosty appearance with an aroma that is a flowery perfume. The flavors are suitably sweet with hints of its grapefruit lineage completing the tangy metallic finish. A nice hybrid high soon follows with a relaxing yet motivational consciousness that's followed by a long-lasting indica stone.

STRAIN NAME

Green Crack ●

TYPE
sativa hybrid ●

LINEAGE
Skunk #1 × (Blue Cheese × Korean Skunk)

SMELL/TASTE
citrus, fruity, floral

COMMON EFFECTS
energized, cheerful, sociable

TOP MEDICINAL USES
fatigue, mood enhancement

AWARD
Emerald Cup

SIMILAR STRAINS
Green Ribbon ● p/196
Blue Dream ● p/94
Super Lemon Haze ● p/358

Originating in the state of Georgia under the name "Cush," Green Crack eventually made its way to the West Coast, where it has since became a popular medical and recreational strain. Green Crack has a pleasant, sweet citrus flavor and an even more pleasant cheerful high. The high is immediate and energized but overconsumption is well known to have a "spacey" and zoned out effect.

STRAIN NAME

Green Ribbon ●

TYPE
hybrid ●

LINEAGE
Green Crack × White Rhino

SMELL/TASTE
fruity, floral, turpentine

COMMON EFFECTS
uplifting, cheerful, sociable

TOP MEDICINAL USES
stress, anxiety

SIMILAR STRAINS
Blue Dream ● p/94
White Widow ● p/386
Afgoo ● p/58

Green Ribbon is a nice strain with a brilliant neon green coloring that shimmers in any light. The resinous buds are thick and dense and give off a pleasantly sweet aroma. The flavor is also subdued but brings in a nice smooth smoke that's easy to take in, allowing for big hits without any harshness. Its effects are a nice hybrid mix that slightly favors the sativa side with a moving energy that will get your body in motion.

STRAIN NAME

Harlequin

TYPE
sativa hybrid ●

LINEAGE
(Colombian Gold × Thai) ×
(Swiss Sativa × Nepal Indica)

SMELL/TASTE
earthy, musky, tropical

COMMON EFFECTS
relaxed, focused, mellow

TOP MEDICINAL USES
pain, stress

AWARD
Medical Cannabis Cup

SIMILAR STRAIN
Cannatonic ● p/122

Harlequin is a medical marijuana marvel. This colorfully dazzling bud is superrich in CBD and its therapeutic effects. This purely medical strain has very low THC levels and has been heralded in the scientific community as a modern-day miracle plant. A major advancement in medical marijuana, Harlequin provides significant medical benefits with very little to no psychoactive effects.

STRAIN NAME

Hash Plant ⬤

TYPE
indica hybrid ●

LINEAGE
Hash Plant × (Hash Plant × Northern Lights)

SMELL/TASTE
peppery, spicy, musky

COMMON EFFECTS
relaxed, cheerful, lazy

TOP MEDICINAL USES
appetite, stress

SIMILAR STRAINS
Romulan ● p/320
Hog's Breath ● p/212
Ingrid ● p/216

———————

Named for its highly resinous buds and hash-like taste, Hash Plant is a world-famous indica. Derived from an original Hash Plant cutting from the Pacific Northwest, it was brought over to Amsterdam in the 1980s and crossbred to create the strong indica we know today. The thick, sharp smoke provides an instant and fast-acting body stone that is extremely long lasting and powerful.

STRAIN NAME

Hawaiian Sativa ●

TYPE
sativa ●

LINEAGE
Landrace (Hawaii)

SMELL/TASTE
citrus, mint, tropical

COMMON EFFECTS
energetic, creative, sociable

TOP MEDICINAL USES
anxiety, mood enhancement

SIMILAR STRAINS
Lamb's Bread ● p/240
Juicy Fruit ● p/230
Island Sweet Skunk ● p/218

From its light green coloring to its long, banana-shaped bud, Hawaiian Sativa is a resin-filled tropical sensation. As with most landrace sativas, this strain has a high-functioning, low-drowsy influence, which is ideal for daytime activities. While the high is energized and sociable, the smoke is light and smooth with a nice mix of tropical fruit flavors. One session with this landrace and you'll understand the true meaning of "da kine."

STRAIN NAME

Haze ●

TYPE
sativa ●

LINEAGE
unknown (California)

SMELL/TASTE
floral, musky, citrus

COMMON EFFECTS
focused, alert, psychedelic

TOP MEDICINAL USES
anxiety, fatigue

AWARDS
Cannabis Cup, Highlife Cup,
Spannabis Cup

SIMILAR STRAINS
Amnesia Haze ● p/70
Cannalope Haze ● p/120
Super Silver Haze ● p/360

Haze is a supersativa believed to be the off-spring of several landrace sativas, including Thai, Mexican, Jamaican, and Colombian varieties. Haze's effects are all cerebral with almost no ceiling to the intense high. Often referred to as "ampheta-weed" for its clear high and alert focus, Haze is a storied strain that dates back to the 1970s, when it originated in Monterey, California. Like all great strains, Haze was eventually brought to Amsterdam, where it was used in a variety of popular crossbreeds, spawning a "Haze Craze."

STRAIN NAME

Head Cheese

TYPE
sativa hybrid ●

LINEAGE
Headband × Cheese

SMELL/TASTE
cheese, fuel, citrus

COMMON EFFECTS
uplifting, relaxing, euphoric

TOP MEDICINAL USES
appetite, stress

SIMILAR STRAINS
Sour Diesel ● p/342
Ogeisel ● p/280
Chiesel ● p/146

This funky sativa hybrid is a superpotent and superpungent strain. Head Cheese is a heavy trichome producer whose glorious crystals are often overshadowed by the powerful fuel-mixed cheese aroma that overwhelms all the senses. The taste is very similar to the aroma with an added kushy undertone that provides a nice complex flavor. The effects are very sativa with an unexpected stoney buzz that relaxes your body without knocking you out with its potent punch.

STRAIN NAME

Headband ●

TYPE
hybrid ●

LINEAGE
Chemdawg ×
(Northern Lights × Super Skunk)

SMELL/TASTE
floral, pine, fuel

COMMON EFFECTS
happy, uplifting, relaxed

TOP MEDICINAL USES
anxiety, stress

AWARDS
Cannabis Cup, Medical Cannabis Cup

SIMILAR STRAINS
Sour Diesel ● p/342
Northern Lights #5 ● p/270
Skywalker ● p/330

———

Headband is known for its well-rounded high—a good mood enhancer, nice body buzz, and not too overpowering. Its lineage gives this hybrid a rich, dense texture with a nice variety of color. The smell is extremely sharp and very "diesel," but the taste is toned down with a sweeter antiseptic-like aftertaste. The effects have a lot of motion, starting with cerebral and then going into physical.
This strain's name refers to the physical and mental head rush that can produce a soothing pressure around the head and face—as if wearing a headband.

STRAIN NAME

Hempstar ●

TYPE
hybrid ●

LINEAGE
Northern Lights × Haze

SMELL/TASTE
earthy, fruity, woody

COMMON EFFECTS
cheerful, focused, relaxed

TOP MEDICINAL USES
stress, anxiety

SIMILAR STRAINS
Atomic Northern Lights ● p/72
G-13 ● p/176
Old Mendo Haze ● p/284

With legendary genetics, Hempstar is a well-balanced, easy-smoking strain. The aromas are very subdued and delicate with a flavor that adds a soft, fruity touch. It is a clean and smooth smoking experience that allows for big hits without coughing. The effects are the real stars of Hempstar, providing a solid, long-lasting happy high that's as clear as it is uplifting. A calming body relaxation rounds out this mild hybrid high.

STRAIN NAME

Hog's Breath ●

TYPE
indica ●

LINEAGE
Hindu Kush × Afghani

SMELL/TASTE
earthy, astringent, pungent

COMMON EFFECTS
body buzz, euphoric, uplifting

TOP MEDICINAL USES
pain, appetite

AWARDS
Cannabis Cup

SIMILAR STRAINS
G-13 ● p/176
Hash Plant ● p/200
LSD ● p/250

The Hog is a potent strain that has its roots in Tennessee. These short, fat buds have a greasy complexion and are covered in gooey resinous trichomes. Its very distinct and dank odor can be misleading as this flower produces a nice smooth and slow-burning smoke. The effects are very indica with an intense full-body buzz, but what makes Hog's Breath so unique is its ability to not cause any of the fatigue typical of such a strong indica.

STRAIN NAME

Holy Grail ●

TYPE
hybrid ●

LINEAGE
Kosher Kush × OG Kush

SMELL/TASTE
pungent, spicy, lemon

COMMON EFFECTS
uplifted, relaxed, cheerful

TOP MEDICINAL USES
stress, pain

AWARDS
Cannabis Cup, Spannabis Cup

SIMILAR STRAINS
BTY OG ● p/110
Kosher Kush ● p/234
Chemdawg ● p/132

This top-rated Kush strain is considered by many to be one of the best hybrids ever cultivated. The dense buds are huge and full of resin, the complex aromas are pungent and powerfully pleasing, and the potent effects are a mellow relaxation balanced with an uplifted cerebral high. Just about every trait of this well-bred strain is as good as it gets, which is why it really is the Holy Grail of Kush.

STRAIN NAME

Ingrid ●

TYPE
indica hybrid ●

LINEAGE
Cheese × Hash Plant

SMELL/TASTE
skunky, musky, metallic

COMMON EFFECTS
relaxed, sleepy, euphoria

TOP MEDICINAL USES
insomnia, muscle tension

SIMILAR STRAINS
Cheese ● p/128
Sugar Shack ● p/356
Chiesel ● p/146

Cheese and Hash Plant may seem like an odd couple but by crossing these two distinct parents, the spiced-cheese aroma of Ingrid is inevitable. Flavor aside, Ingrid is a heavy-hitting indica that provides a powerful, stoney high. These thick, dense buds also carry a very unique trichome covering that make them ideal for producing cannabis concentrates.

STRAIN NAME

Island Sweet Skunk ●

TYPE
sativa hybrid ●

LINEAGE
Skunk #1 × unknown (Canada)

SMELL/TASTE
sweet, pungent, fruity

COMMON EFFECTS
euphoria, mellow, cheerful

TOP MEDICINAL USES
stress, anxiety

AWARDS
Medical Cannabis Cup

SIMILAR STRAINS
Hawaiian Sativa ● p/202
LSD ● p/250
Black Tuna ● p/84

Originating from Vancouver Island, Canada, Island Sweet Skunk is a sticky, sweet skunk sensation. The Sweet Skunk appears bright orange in complexion with its twisting orange hairs and glowing amber crystals. The smoke is heavy and lung expanding, producing an uplifting euphoria that mellows out into a nice carefree and sustainable high. It's no wonder that Sweet Skunk has been a staple strain in Canada for decades.

STRAIN NAME

J1

TYPE
sativa hybrid ●

LINEAGE
Jack Herer × Skunk #1

SMELL/TASTE
citrus, sweet, minty

COMMON EFFECTS
energetic, uplifting, euphoria

TOP MEDICINAL USES
fatigue, mood enhancement

SIMILAR STRAINS
XJ-13 ● p/388
Jack the Ripper ● p/224
Trainwreck ● p/372

This top-shelf sativa was made for the wake and bake session. These frosty buds have a dense, stacked structure with an aroma that mixes the best of both parents, resulting in a citrusy mint combined with a sharp sweetness that only gets more aromatic as you break it up in anticipation of what's to come. The flavor is similar to the smell with a pleasant, spicy aftertaste that comes as you exhale, which is ultrasmooth. The effects come on fast with an uplifting rush that will send your mind floating throughout the enduring high.

STRAIN NAME

Jack Herer

TYPE
sativa ●

LINEAGE
(Northern Lights #5 × Haze) ×
Skunk #1

SMELL/TASTE
sweet, lemony, zesty

COMMON EFFECTS
energetic, alert, happy

TOP MEDICINAL USES
anxiety, stress

AWARDS
Cannabis Cup, Highlife Cup, Medical
Cannabis Cup, Spannabis Cup

SIMILAR STRAINS
XJ-13 ● p/388
J1 ● p/220
Jack the Ripper ● p/224

The late great Jack Herer ("The Emperor of Hemp") is considered the father of marijuana legalization, and this prized sativa-dominant strain lives up to his honor. This crystal-laden nugget provides a clean, fresh taste and is an extremely popular daytime strain, thanks in part to its smooth smoke and uplifting, clear-headed high that grows and then kindly eases away with no crash and burn. Its sharp flavors and immediate long-lasting high make Jack Herer a highly coveted strain.

Jack Herer was an activist and writer whose 1985 book The Emperor Wears No Clothes *helped spark the modern-era cannabis legalization movement. His belief that cannabis should be used legally as a fiber, fuel, food, and medicine continues to gain support from states across the country. He died on April 15, 2010, but his legacy still lives on.*

STRAIN NAME

Jack the Ripper

TYPE
sativa hybrid ●

LINEAGE
Space Queen × Jack's Cleaner

SMELL/TASTE
lemon, piney, mango

COMMON EFFECTS
psychedelic, energetic, uplifted

TOP MEDICINAL USES
pain, appetite

SIMILAR STRAINS
Durban Poison ● p/166
Jack Herer ● p/222
Super Lemon Haze ● p/358

The sativa influence on Jack the Ripper is obvious at fist glance. This elongated spear-like bud structure is a telltale sign of a well-grown Jack the Ripper strain. With lemony smells and tart flavors, this "killer" strain rips hard and fast, producing a motivating energy that continues to creep throughout the high.

STRAIN NAME

Jack Skellington ●

TYPE
hybrid ●

LINEAGE
Jack the Ripper ×
(Cinderella 99 × G-13)

SMELL/TASTE
citrus, astringent, fruity

COMMON EFFECTS
euphoria, alert, creative

TOP MEDICINAL USES
stress, anxiety

SIMILAR STRAINS
Trainwreck ● p/372
Jack Herer ● p/222
J1 ● p/220

The copious amounts of resin found in this bud make Jack Skellington one of the best resin-producing plants in the cannabis world. And with all those crystals comes intense and mind-numbing potency that provides immediate euphoria combined with a sharp focus and clarity. But don't let the tempting citrus flavors make you overindulge, this powerhouse strain is a one-hit wonder that needs to be respected.

STRAIN NAME

Jillybean ●

TYPE
hybrid ●

LINEAGE
Space Queen × Orange Velvet

SMELL/TASTE
citrus, candy, fruity

COMMON EFFECTS
uplifting, cheerful, body buzz

TOP MEDICINAL USES
mood enhancement, stress

AWARD
Cannabis Cup

SIMILAR STRAINS
Tangie ● p/370
Cinderella 99 ● p/148
MTF ● p/266

The dense, deep burgundy buds of Jillybean give off an enticing dank orange aroma that just begins to express the complex flavor profiles within. Jillybean is one of those strains that should be puffed through a vaporizer to really appreciate all its wonderful fruity flavors, which range from tangy orange, to sweet mango, to candied apple. The resulting high is a perfect hybrid of a mellow stone with a clearhead high.

STRAIN NAME

Juicy Fruit ●

TYPE
hybrid ●

LINEAGE
Thai × Afghani

SMELL/TASTE
fruity, sweet, floral

COMMON EFFECTS
sociable, cheerful, body buzz

TOP MEDICINAL USES
mood enhancement, anxiety

SIMILAR STRAINS
Champagne ● p/126
Super Lemon Haze ● p/358
Blackberry ● p/86

———

Juicy Fruit is the ideal fusion of two polar opposite ends of the cannabis world—Thai sativa and Afghani indica. The bud's full spectrum of green to lavender colors radiate from the thick trichome crystals that cover its plump structure. The intense fruity flavors produce a dizzying sweet smoke that fills your head with a refreshing boost of jubilation while filling your body with a head-to-toe tingle. Juicy Fruit is a perfectly balanced and immaculate hybrid.

STRAIN NAME

King's Bread ●

TYPE
sativa ●

LINEAGE
Landrace (Jamaica)

SMELL/TASTE
citrus, tropical, minty

COMMON EFFECTS
euphoria, uplifted, cheerful

TOP MEDICINAL USES
appetite, stress

SIMILAR STRAINS
Lamb's Bread ● p/240
Jack Herer ● p/222
Hawaiian Sativa ● p/202

King's Bread, or King's Breath, is thought to be a royal parent to the legendary Lamb's Bread strain, both hailing from Jamaica, the island well known for producing great ganja. This tropical flower has a classic sativa bud structure with a remarkably pungent citrus scent. The smoke is crisp and light, provoking a mellow high that can only be described as "irie."

STRAIN NAME

Kosher Kush ●

TYPE
indica hybrid ●

LINEAGE
unknown (California)

SMELL/TASTE
earthy, sweet, fruity

COMMON EFFECTS
relaxed, body buzz, spacey

TOP MEDICINAL USES
insomnia, appetite

AWARDS
Cannabis Cup, Medical Cannabis
Cup, Spannabis Cup

SIMILAR STRAINS
Holy Grail ● p/214
BTY OG ● p/110
XXX OG ● p/390

Originally called Jew's Gold or JG for short, this OG Kush hybrid is famous for its unbelievable THC and CBD levels. Shrouded in lore and mystery, demand for this powerful medicine quickly spread throughout California, requiring a more universal and nonsecular name. The name Kosher Kush also pays homage to the original Jewish growers as well as the strain's unique flavor. The high cannabinoid levels produce a heavy-hitting indica strain that is said to make your body feel "blessed" with total relaxation and euphoria.

STRAIN NAME

Kryptonite ●

TYPE
indica hybrid ●

LINEAGE
unknown

SMELL/TASTE
fruity, skunky, sweet

COMMON EFFECTS
body buzz, relaxed, alert

TOP MEDICINAL USES
pain, muscle tension

SIMILAR STRAINS
Cinderella 99 ● p/148
Grape Ape ● p/190
G-13 ● p/176

Just one look at this awe-inspiring bud and you can already begin to feel the power of this frosty treat. Kryptonite will hit you faster than a speeding bullet with a body buzz more powerful than a locomotive. The relaxing body high is accompanied by an alert, cloud-free mind, making this indica hybrid a favorite choice for pain relief in the medical marijuana community.

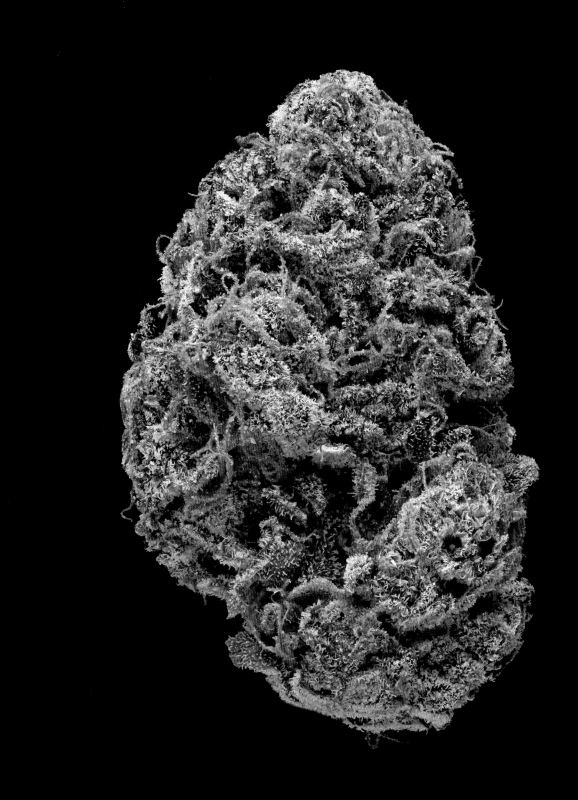

STRAIN NAME

LA Confidential●

TYPE
indica●

LINEAGE
Afghani × California Afghani

SMELL/TASTE
sweet, piney, nutty

COMMON EFFECTS
couch-lock, body buzz, sleepy

AWARDS
Cannabis Cup

TOP MEDICINAL USES
insomnia, pain

SIMILAR STRAINS
Master Kush ● p/256
Pure Gold ● p/304
Skywalker ● p/330

LA Confidential, a.k.a. Con or Conny, is a very popular and all-around standout strain. It's easy to grow, looks amazing, has a classic old-school flavor, and affects your body with a deep relaxation. The effects, come on almost immediately, making LA Confidential a common "one-hitter-quitter." After this thick smoke clears, be prepared to just chill and relax because you won't be able to do much of anything else.

STRAIN NAME

Lamb's Bread

TYPE
sativa

LINEAGE
Landrace (Jamaica)

SMELL/TASTE
spicy, earthy, citrus

COMMON EFFECTS
creative, happy, energetic

TOP MEDICINAL USES
stress, anxiety

SIMILAR STRAINS
King's Bread p/232
Congolese Sativa p/150
Hawaiian Sativa p/202

The name of this tropical sativa, Lamb's Bread, is often used in Jamaican culture and music as a proverb to express marijuana's effects and abilities. And the ability of this strain to give you an uplifting head rush is second to none. Lamb's Bread hits you with a sense of such creativity and inspiration it's no wonder the immortal Bob Marley sang songs of its praise. A few hits in the morning will have you smiling at the rising sun and not worrying about a thing.

STRAIN NAME
Larry OG

TYPE
hybrid ●

LINEAGE
OG Kush phenotype

SMELL/TASTE
lemon, menthol, fuel

COMMON EFFECTS
relaxed, body buzz, cheerful

TOP MEDICINAL USES
pain, appetite

AWARDS
Cannabis Cup
Medical Cannabis Cup

SIMILAR STRAINS
LA Confidential ● p/238
Platinum OG ● p/298
True OG ● p/376

Larry OG is a more indica-dominant version of the OG Kush family of hybrids. This lemon-fueled pheno is caked in resin, making it one of the stickiest, heavy-hitting OGs. Larry's high THC levels make for a potent indica body-high that is highly sought after by medical marijuana users. Both medical and recreational users will appreciate Larry's ability to keep the buzz going long and strong without any laziness or sleepiness.

STRAIN NAME

Lavender ●

TYPE
indica hybrid ●

LINEAGE
Afghani-Hawaiian × (Super Skunk × Korean Skunk)

SMELL/TASTE
floral, skunky, tropical

COMMON EFFECTS
Relaxed, euphoria, body buzz

TOP MEDICINAL USES
pain, muscle tension

AWARDS
Cannabis Cup, Spannabis Cup, Highlife Cup

SIMILAR STRAINS
GDP ● p/178
Grape Ape ● p/190
Sour Grape ● p/346

Bringing together some world power genetics, Lavender is a cornucopia of color, flavor, and effects. Saturated purples, vibrant oranges, neon greens, and frosty whites fill the bud's stacked structure. The lovely flowery perfume gives this strain its namesake with a flavor to match. The smoke is deceptively dense and hits with a heavy full-body stone that seems to slow the world down.

STRAIN NAME

Lemon Skunk ●

TYPE
sativa hybrid ●

LINEAGE
unknown (Las Vegas)

SMELL/TASTE
lemon, minty, skunky

COMMON EFFECTS
euphoria, relaxed, mellow

TOP MEDICINAL USES
appetite, stress

AWARDS
Emerald Cup, Highlife Cup,
Spannabis Cup

SIMILAR STRAINS
Super Lemon Haze ● p/358
Trainwreck ● p/372
Jack Herer ● p/222

This bicultural strain is a cross between two unknown Skunk strains, the product of an old mother plant hailing from Las Vegas, and a prized father from Holland. Lemon Skunk's light green buds grow long and tall and ooze golden-yellow trichome crystals. The smell of zesty lemons dominates the aromas, while the flavor adds a minty burst of freshness. The heavy-hitting sativa high will have you soaring with a mellow relaxation that will keep you from spacing out.

STRAIN NAME

Louis XIII ●

TYPE
hybrid ●

LINEAGE
OG Kush phenotype

SMELL/TASTE
piney, floral, earthy

COMMON EFFECTS
body buzz, euphoria, spacey

TOP MEDICINAL USES
pain, stress

SIMILAR STRAINS
Ghost ● p/180
Abusive OG ● p/54
Triangle ● p/374

————

Louis XIII, a.k.a. King Louis, is the royal cut of OG Kush. The dense, dark green nugs and short, fiery red hairs are true to its roots, while its flavor adds a nice flowery spice to its old-school kush taste. The smoke is slow burning and heavy hitting with an overwhelming pine aroma. The King's strong body high creeps throughout the high, while the euphoric clear head will make you feel like part of a super-high society.

STRAIN NAME

LSD ●

TYPE
indica hybrid ●

LINEAGE
Mazar × Skunk #1

SMELL/TASTE
earthy, sweet, nutty

COMMON EFFECTS
body buzz, euphoria, cheerful

TOP MEDICINAL USES
pain, nausea

AWARDS
Cannabis Cup

SIMILAR STRAINS
Hog's Breath ● p/212
Berry White ● p/74
Bio Diesel ● p/78

———————

The "all-natural" aromas and nutty sweet smoke of LSD make you feel as if you're having a session with Mother Nature herself. While the name LSD may seem a bit too trippy for this strain, her mind-altering effects are definitely impressive for an indica hybrid. The body high is first-class while the euphoric sensations are very stimulating and make for an enjoyable full mind-and-body experience.

STRAIN NAME

Lucid Dream

TYPE
sativa hybrid ●

LINEAGE
Blue Dream × Amnesia Haze

SMELL/TASTE
sweet, floral, fruity

COMMON EFFECTS
uplifting, cheerful, creative

TOP MEDICINAL USES
appetite, mood enhancement

SIMILAR STRAINS
Green Ribbon ● p/196
Blue Kush ● p/98
Trainwreck ● p/372

The dream team genetics behind this sativa cross results in a strain that truly makes you feel like you're living in a dream. Lucid Dream's appearance is divine with its green-to-purple hues and nicely contrasting hairs that scatter throughout an uplifted stature that glistens in pure white resin. Its sweet smoke hits smooth and leads into a strong sativa high that's a dreamy wonder. Lucid Dream is a perfect daytime strain for any creative activity.

STRAIN NAME

Martian Candy ●

TYPE
indica hybrid ●

LINEAGE
unknown

SMELL/TASTE
fruity, sweet, spicy

COMMON EFFECTS
body buzz, relaxed, alert

TOP MEDICINAL USES
pain, insomnia

SIMILAR STRAINS
Snocap ● p/332
Bubble Gum ● p/114
Burkle ● p/116

The fat buds of Martian Candy are a nice sticky treat that break up into perfectly sized morsels begging to be rolled up. The aromas are a pleasant mix of fruity sweetness, and the flavor adds a kick of spice to the candy-like taste. Although Martian Candy's genetics are unknown, the mellow, full-body buzz is a clear indicator of its indica roots, while the clear head adds a nice hybrid touch.

STRAIN NAME

Master Kush ●

TYPE
indica ●

LINEAGE
Hindu Kush Afghani × Hindu Kush
Afghani

SMELL/TASTE
pungent, skunky, earthy

COMMON EFFECTS
euphoria, relaxed, body buzz

TOP MEDICINAL USES
pain, stress

AWARDS
Cannabis Cup, Highlife Cup

SIMILAR STRAINS
LA Confidential ● p/238
Bubba Kush ● p/112
Afghani ● p/56

Master Kush was born by crossing two unique strains from opposite ends of the Hindu Kush region of central Asia. The resulting Master Kush strain is a dank and resinous flower with an exotic earthy aroma and pungent flavors. The strong indica effects come with a bright mental clarity not typical with such a potent full-body melt. These plump, fat flowers are well known for their friendly growing habits, making Master Kush a popular strain for growers of all skill levels.

STRAIN NAME

Maui Waui

TYPE
sativa

LINEAGE
Landrace (Hawaii)

SMELL/TASTE
tropical, fruity, astringent

COMMON EFFECTS
euphoria, mellow, cheerful

TOP MEDICINAL USES
stress, appetite

SIMILAR STRAINS
Super Lemon Haze p/358
Afgoo p/58
Afwreck p/60

This classic landrace strain is a true all-star sativa. It grows fluffy and tall with the traditional citrus aromas you'd expect from an island-grown sativa. The smoke is light with a unique tropical fruity flavor. The sativa high is surprisingly mellow with an amazing uplifting experience full of gentle energy, instant happiness, focused creativity, and it is simply inspiring.

STRAIN NAME

Michael Phelps ●

TYPE
indica hybrid ●

LINEAGE
unknown (California)

SMELL/TASTE
citrus, fuel, lemon

COMMON EFFECTS
focus, relaxed, mellow

TOP MEDICINAL USES
anxiety, nausea

SIMILAR STRAINS
Tahoe OG ● p/368
SFV OG ● p/324
True OG ● p/376

Michael Phelps is an OG Kush mix of unknown origins. This incredibly dense and chunky flower wins the gold medal in appearance with its old-school Kush bud structure that swims in gooey crystals. With a name like Michael Phelps, you better believe this strain will hit you in record time with a well-focused head high and an uplifting body tranquility that feels like you're floating on water.

STRAIN NAME

Motorbreath

TYPE
sativa hybrid ●

LINEAGE
Chemdawg × SFV OG

SMELL/TASTE
piney, citrus, fuel

COMMON EFFECTS
uplifting, body buzz, spacey

TOP MEDICINAL USES
pain, stress

SIMILAR STRAINS
Sour Diesel ● p/342
Michael Phelps ● p/260
Ghost ● p/180

The timeless OG smells and Chemdawg flavors make this bud a great puff. This bud burns slow and hits with a fuel-filled exhale that gives this strain its awesome name. The thick smoke gives way to a sedative buzz that's mellow and soothing. A spacey cerebral high creeps in and takes over the high, making Motorbreath a very potent sativa mix.

STRAIN NAME

Mr. Nice Guy ●

TYPE
indica ●

LINEAGE
G–13 × Hash Plant

SMELL/TASTE
sweet, earthy, citrus

COMMON EFFECTS
body buzz, relaxing, lazy

TOP MEDICINAL USES
pain, stress

SIMILAR STRAINS
GDP ● p/178
God's Gift ● p/186
Lavender ● p/244

The mottled coloring of Mr. Nice Guy beautifully encompasses the full gamut of wonderful cannabis colors. Topped off with a golden resin coat, this powerhouse indica is sure to pack a superpotent punch. Its flavors are a pleasant mixture of sweet and tangy with a spiced earth overtone, making for a tasty hash-like smoke. A serious stone will creep in after just a few puffs and intensify into a very "nice" body high.

STRAIN NAME

MTF

TYPE
hybrid ●

LINEAGE
unknown (Alaska)

SMELL/TASTE
fruity, musky, creamy

COMMON EFFECTS
uplifting, euphoria, body buzz

TOP MEDICINAL USES
stress, pain

SIMILAR STRAINS
Northern Lights #5 ● p/270
Jillybean ● p/228
Skunk #1 ● p/328

MTF (also known as Matanuska Thunderfuck or Alaskan Thunder Fuck) originally hails from the Matanuska Valley just north of Anchorage, Alaska. A very popular strain from the 1970s, MTF is a monster bud with a sweet, creamy flavor that hits big with a creeping stone that comes on slow and intensifies into a heavy buzz just as the cerebral head high takes effect. These full-hybrid effects are powerful and long lasting, so puff this Alaskan legend with discretion.

STRAIN NAME

Northern Blueberry ●

TYPE
indica ●

LINEAGE
Northern Lights × Blueberry

SMELL/TASTE
berry, fruity, earthy

COMMON EFFECTS
body buzz, relaxing, euphoria

TOP MEDICINAL USES
pain, stress

SIMILAR STRAINS
Blue Kush ● p/98
Goo Berry ● p/188
Romulan Berry ● p/322

————

The Blueberry strain's flavor and genetics are a perfect complement to the legendary Northern Lights. Northern Blueberry is a compact and thick flower with appetizing blue and purple highlights that bleed a delicate berry aroma. The stoney high is all indica powered with an intense euphoria that stretches through your entire body and head, adding a nice cerebral balance.

STRAIN NAME

Northern Lights #5 ●

TYPE
indica ●

LINEAGE
unknown (California indica × Afghani)
× (Skunk #1 × Haze)

SMELL/TASTE
lemon, sweet, piney

COMMON EFFECTS
lazy, relaxed, mellow

TOP MEDICINAL USES
pain

AWARDS
Cannabis Cup, Highlife Cup,
Spannabis Cup

SIMILAR STRAINS
Afghani ● p/56
Burkle ● p/116
God's Gift ● p/186

Northern Lights is a dominant and pure indica that originates from the Pacific Northwest but was made famous in Holland. It has received worldwide recognition and its genetics are used as the basis for many of the best hybrids grown today. It was believed that there were originally a total of eleven original Northern Lights plants labeled #1 through #11, with the #5 plant considered the best overall specimen. The buds are sticky and dense and the physical stone is a full-body buzz, making Northern Lights *the* model example of what an indica should be—worthy of its reputation as one of the world's best indicas.

STRAIN NAME

Nuken ●

TYPE
indica hybrid ●

LINEAGE
God Bud × Kish

SMELL/TASTE
sweet, floral, creamy

COMMON EFFECTS
relaxed, euphoria, alert

TOP MEDICINAL USES
muscle tension, appetite

SIMILAR STRAINS
Atomic Northern Lights ● p/72
Blackberry Kush ● p/88
Big Buddha Cheese ● p/76

This Canadian flower bomb is a weapon of massive THC. Nuken's aroma is a stealthy, floral bouquet that leads to a tasty sweet cream flavor. The silky smooth smoke gives way to a full-body meltdown that pulses through every muscle. The stone is long and strong, but your mind will be pleasantly clear and wide-awake, giving this explosive indica hybrid a slight hybrid balance.

STRAIN NAME

NYC Diesel

TYPE
sativa hybrid ●

LINEAGE
Mexican Sativa × Afghani

SMELL/TASTE
grapefruit, lemon, exotic

COMMON EFFECTS
energetic, alert, sociable

TOP MEDICINAL USES
fatigue, appetite

AWARDS
Cannabis Cup, Highlife Cup, Medical
Cannabis Cup

SIMILAR STRAINS
Daywrecker ● p/158
Headband ● p/208
Chemdawg ● p/132

NYC Diesel is yet another standout strain from the infamous Diesel family. With its roots based in the city that never sleeps, this sativa-dominant hybrid will awake your mind with a euphoric and energized high. NYC buds are dense, dank, and truly diesel with their fuel-inspired aromas that fill the room. The flavors will coat your palate with an exotic lemon-lime taste that finishes with a distinct grapefruit tang.

STRAIN NAME

Obama OG ●

hybrid ●

LINEAGE
(Skunk #1 × unknown) ×
(OG Kush × Afghani)

SMELL/TASTE
piney, nutty, musty

COMMON EFFECTS
uplifting, cheerful, relaxed

TOP MEDICINAL USES
stress, anxiety

SIMILAR STRAINS
Abusive OG ● p/54
Michael Phelps ● p/260
Louis XIII ● p/248

———

Named in honor of the POTUS, Obama OG is a complex kush hybrid that is a bipartisan mix of its indica and sativa roots. The frosty bud aromas and flavors are not overpowering and offer a well-balanced high that will stimulate the mind and soothe the body.

"I don't think it (marijuana) is more dangerous than alcohol." —President Obama

"When I was a kid, I inhaled frequently. That was the point." —President Obama

STRAIN NAME

OG Kush ●

TYPE
hybrid ●

LINEAGE
ChemDawg × (Lemon Thai × Hindu Kush)

SMELL/TASTE
sweet, citrus, fuel

COMMON EFFECTS
euphoria, relaxed, cheerful

TOP MEDICINAL USES
pain, stress

AWARDS
Highlife Cup, Medical Cannabis Cup, Spannabis Cup

SIMILAR STRAINS
Sour Diesel ● p/342
SFV OG ● p/324
BTY OG ● p/110

OG Kush and its phenotypes are perhaps the most common cannabis variety available today. This legendary strain originated out of Southern California in the mid 1990s. While the genetics of OG Kush are heavily debated, its popularity is undeniable. The dense little nuggets have a classic sweet-and-sour flavor. Coupled with a long-lasting and powerful body buzz and euphoric mind state, it's no wonder OG Kush has risen to such high demand. Various growers have used cuttings from the OG plant to grow popular phenotypes of their own—spawning an OG craze throughout California and gaining mythical stature.

STRAIN NAME

Ogiesel ●

TYPE
hybrid ●

LINEAGE
OG Kush × Sour Diesel

SMELL/TASTE
acrid, fuel, citrus

COMMON EFFECTS
energetic, cheerful, sociable

TOP MEDICINAL USES
stress, mood enhancement

SIMILAR STRAINS
Chiesel ● p/146
NYC Diesel ● p/274
Girl Scout Cookies ● p/182

It was only a matter of time before the East Coast Diesel and the West Coast OG made a superhybrid love child. These world-class parents bring a strong mix of lemony fuel-charged aromas and flavors that will please any toker's palate. Ogiesel's high starts with a sativa kick that will uplift your emotions and energize your mind. A creeping mellow body relaxation nicely rounds out the hybrid high, making Ogiesel a great anytime strain.

STRAIN NAME

Ogre

TYPE
indica hybrid ●

LINEAGE
Master Kush × Bubba Kush

SMELL/TASTE
skunky, citrus, lemon

COMMON EFFECTS
sleepy, relaxed, body buzz

TOP MEDICINAL USES
insomnia, pain

SIMILAR STRAINS
XXX OG ● p/390
Tahoe OG ● p/368
Platinum OG ● p/298

Powerful indica genetics give this dank bud a monster appeal. This beast of a bud has traditional kush flavors and aromas with a skunkier kick than its predecessors. But what really makes Ogre so powerful is its potent physical effects which produce a knockout punch that will put you into a deep, stoney trance.

STRAIN NAME

Old Mendo Haze

TYPE
sativa●

LINEAGE
Haze phenotype

SMELL/TASTE
piney, minty, spicy

COMMON EFFECTS
psychedelic, creative, energetic

TOP MEDICINAL USES
mood enhancement, fatigue

SIMILAR STRAINS
Mr. Nice Guy● p/264
Haze● p/204
Super Silver Haze● p/360

Old Mendo Haze is an eye-popping Haze pheno hailing from the fabled Mendocino County of the Emerald Triangle. Old Mendo Haze is a well-rounded example that delivers the complete head-to-toe buzz and racing mind energy Haze is known and loved for.

The Emerald Triangle consists of Mendocino County, Humboldt County, and Trinity County. This region of Northern California has been cultivating marijuana since the 1960s and is one of the largest cannabis-producing areas in the United States.

STRAIN NAME

P91 ●

TYPE
sativa hybrid ●

LINEAGE
Thai × (Thai × [Thai × Afghani])

SMELL/TASTE
citrus, aloe, peppery, floral

COMMON EFFECTS
cheerful, uplifted, euphoria

TOP MEDICINAL USES
anxiety, depression

SIMILAR STRAINS
Blackberry Kush ● p/88
Amnesia Haze ● p/70
Romulan ● p/320

———————

P91 is a strain that came out of Poway County ("P") in northern San Diego, California, back in 1991 ("91"). Its fabled history is riddled with stories of the early West Coast grow scene, but what is known for certain about this sativa-dominated strain is that it has a very distinct flavor and its psychoactive effects are fast acting. Although the experience may seem fleeting, it is definitely a highly concentrated high that can get pretty psychedelic at times.

STRAIN NAME

Panama Red ●

TYPE
sativa ●

LINEAGE
Landrace (Panama)

SMELL/TASTE
pungent, earthy, musky

COMMON EFFECTS
energetic, uplifting, cheerful

TOP MEDICINAL USES
fatigue, mood enhancement

AWARDS
Medical Cannabis Cup

SIMILAR STRAINS
Congolese Sativa ● p/150
Red Congo ● p/316
Maui Waui ● p/258

Panama Red is a legendary landrace ganja immortalized in song and story dating back to the 1960s. Panama Red is one of the first "brand names" ever given to a cannabis strain and along with its rival Acapulco Gold set the stage for the strain-naming frenzy of today. The fiery red hairs are the signature feature of this flower and the happy head high is what keeps Panama Red a throwback that continues to gain popularity with anyone who's smoked the Red.

STRAIN NAME

Pineapple ●

TYPE
sativa hybrid ●

LINEAGE
unknown (California)

SMELL/TASTE
pineapple, earthy, lemon

COMMON EFFECTS
euphoria, spacey, uplifting

TOP MEDICINAL USES
mood enhancement, appetite

AWARD
Emerald Cup

SIMILAR STRAINS
Tangie ● p/370
Pineapple Express ● p/292
Agent Orange ● p/62

This sticky, fluffy indulgence produces a quality smoke with a strong sativa kick. The tangy pineapple-lemon aromas and flavors burst in your mouth with a subtle floral bouquet to round out the delightful taste. Pineapple's nice strong head high will uplift your emotions with bursts of electric energy that sets your mind buzzing and thoughts racing. Pineapple's effects make it very hard to focus attention on anything other than feeling great.

STRAIN NAME

Pineapple Express

TYPE
sativa hybrid ●

LINEAGE
Trainwreck × Hawaiian Sativa

SMELL/TASTE
pineapple, tropical, spicy

COMMON EFFECTS
uplifting, energetic, creative

TOP MEDICINAL USES
stress, mood enhancement

SIMILAR STRAINS
Island Sweet Skunk ● p/218
Kryptonite ● p/236
Pineapple ● p/290

The visual appeal of Pineapple Express is only surpassed by its astonishing taste and smell. The aroma is a delicate mix of fruity tropical sensations, while the sweet flavor is unmistakably pineapple with a subtle, spicy aftertaste. The flower's intense resin produces a smoke that is thick and expansive—immediately generating an energetic high that lasts for hours. Pineapple Express is an all-around high-quality cannabis that makes a fantastic daytime treat.

STRAIN NAME

Pink Pearl ●

TYPE
hybrid ●

LINEAGE
White Ribbon × Cherry Pie

SMELL/TASTE
fruity, buttery, pungent

COMMON EFFECTS
uplifting, euphoria, relaxing

TOP MEDICINAL USES
stress, appetite

SIMILAR STRAINS
Tangie ● p/370
Girl Scout Cookies ● p/182
Hempstar ● p/210

Pink Pearl has a very complex aroma and flavor profile that combines buttery popcorn, fruity melon, and a pungent spice into one crazy and oddly appetizing taste. The golden trichomes bring out a smooth, stoney high with an even-keeled energy that's counter balanced with a mellow physical stone. Pink Pearl is sure to please any discerning toker with its full range of effects and flavors.

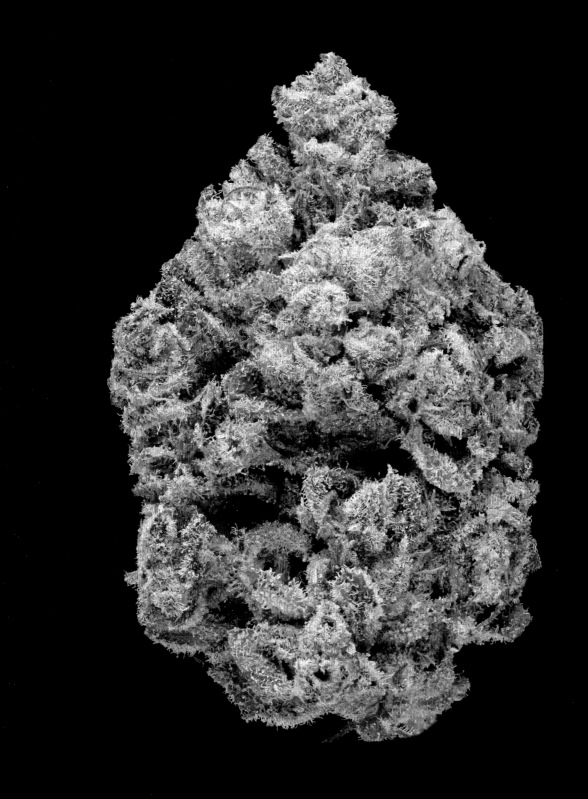

STRAIN NAME

Platinum Bubba●

TYPE
indica ●

LINEAGE
OG Kush × Bubba Kush

SMELL/TASTE
musky, skunky, creamy

COMMON EFFECTS
euphoria, cheerful, relaxed

TOP MEDICINAL USES
appetite, nausea

SIMILAR STRAINS
Master Kush ● p/256
Pre-98 Bubba ● p/300
Platinum OG ● p/298

Platinum Bubba is a classic indica that will leave you happy, hungry, and relaxed. The remarkable frosty green coloring of this bud is set afire by the insane red hairs that shoot off from it. The heavy high starts in the head and moves right through your body, causing a serious case of the "munchies." After the snack session is complete, Platinum Bubba's deep relaxation will take over, putting you into serious nap-time mode.

STRAIN NAME

Platinum OG ●

TYPE
hybrid ●

LINEAGE
OG Kush phenotype

SMELL/TASTE
musky, nutty, floral

COMMON EFFECTS
relaxed, lazy, mellow

TOP MEDICINAL USES
pain, appetite

SIMILAR STRAINS
XXX OG ● p/390
Ghost ● p/180
SFV OG ● p/324

Another amazing OG Kush phenotype, this specimen offers silvery crystals smothered on big, stacked buds. This particular OG provides a smooth, buttery smoke that tastes like sweet pine nuts. Its head-to-toe stress relief warms your body like a comfortable blanket, while putting your head in a good space. Platinum OG is another flawless example of how an OG Kush should perform.

STRAIN NAME

Pre-98 Bubba ●

TYPE
indica ●

LINEAGE
OG Kush × (West Coast Dog × Old World Kush)

SMELL/TASTE
earthy, creamy, skunky

COMMON EFFECTS
euphoria, relaxed, sleepy

TOP MEDICINAL USES
insomnia, appetite

AWARDS
Medical Cannabis Cup

SIMILAR STRAINS
Bubba Kush ● p/112
Master Kush ● p/256
Platinum Bubba ● p/296

Although no relation to Bubba Kush, Pre-98 Bubba borrows the name as an homage to the original Bubba. Its classic old-school looks with dank greens and reds nicely complement this buds skunky kush aromas. The smoke is very thick with a creamy aftertaste. A perfect chill out stone, Pre-98 Bubba affects the body with a calming euphoria resulting in a relaxing state of mind.

STRAIN NAME

Presidential OG ●

TYPE
indica hybrid ●

LINEAGE
Bubble Gum × OG Kush

SMELL/TASTE
earthy, piney, sweet

COMMON EFFECTS
mellow, focused

TOP MEDICINAL USES
insomnia, stress, pain

AWARDS
Cannabis Cup

SIMILAR STRAINS
Purple OG ● p/310
Querkle ● p/314
Sour LA ● p/348

Presidential OG is a contemporary kush hybrid that is mostly indica based, although its effects are unmistakably cerebral. Its inbred sedative nature will hit you quickly, while feelings of being alert and focused nicely balance out the stoney high. Like a good president, this is a popular all-around strain that tries to please all parties.

Founding Fathers

"We shall, by and by, want a world of hemp more for our own consumption." —John Adams

"Hemp is of first necessity to the wealth and protection of the country." —Thomas Jefferson

"Make the most of the Indian hemp seed, and sow it everywhere!" —George Washington

STRAIN NAME

Pure Gold ●

TYPE
indica hybrid ●

LINEAGE
unknown

SMELL/TASTE
vanilla, fruity, skunky

COMMON EFFECTS
relaxed, spacey, couch-lock

TOP MEDICINAL USES
appetite, muscle tension

SIMILAR STRAINS
Kosher Kush ● p/234
Super Skunk ● p/364
Crystal Coma ● p/156

The gnarly yarn-like orange hairs on Pure Gold drip syrupy trichomes that endow this tight little flower with a golden shine. The taste and aroma are much less pronounced than its appearance, but they have a sweet vanilla tinge that hits with a skunky aftertaste. The indica power is definitely present in Pure Gold and induces a strong couch-like effect. Expect a spacey head high that mellows out as you drift into full-body relaxation.

STRAIN NAME
Purple Alien OG ●

TYPE
hybrid ●

LINEAGE
Las Vegas Purple Kush × Alien OG

SMELL/TASTE
grape, fruity, spicy

COMMON EFFECTS
relaxed, energetic, mellow

TOP MEDICINAL USES
muscle tension, stress

SIMILAR STRAINS
Black Cherry Soda ● p/80
Purple Sticky Punch ● p/312
Purple OG ● p/310

Purple Alien OG is a sneaky little hybrid. The aromas are very subtle but the toke packs a big, fruity flavor and hits superhard and fast. The immediate downward body relaxation starts off mellow before an unexpected energy rush sneaks up and sets your mind into high drive. The roller-coaster effects continue as the adrenaline rush subsides and a full-body stone takes over for the remainder of the ride.

STRAIN NAME

Purple Dawg ●

TYPE
indica hybrid ●

LINEAGE
Grape Train Kush × Star Dawg

SMELL/TASTE
earthy, fruity, sweet

COMMON EFFECTS
body buzz, relaxed, sleepy

TOP MEDICINAL USES
insomnia, pain

SIMILAR STRAINS
Purple Sticky Punch ● p/312
Sour Grape ● p/346
Euphoria ● p/170

Purple Dawg has some of the darkest and deepest colors of any strain. The purples seem to turn almost black with a resin so thick it makes the flower appear to be dipped in honey. The flavors are surprisingly mellow for such a colorful bud, but what Purple Dawg lacks in taste it more than makes up for in effects. The deep and pulsing body buzz creeps in but kicks hard once it does. The sedative sensations overwhelm any cerebral effects that try to slip in, making this indica hybrid a real couch-locking stone.

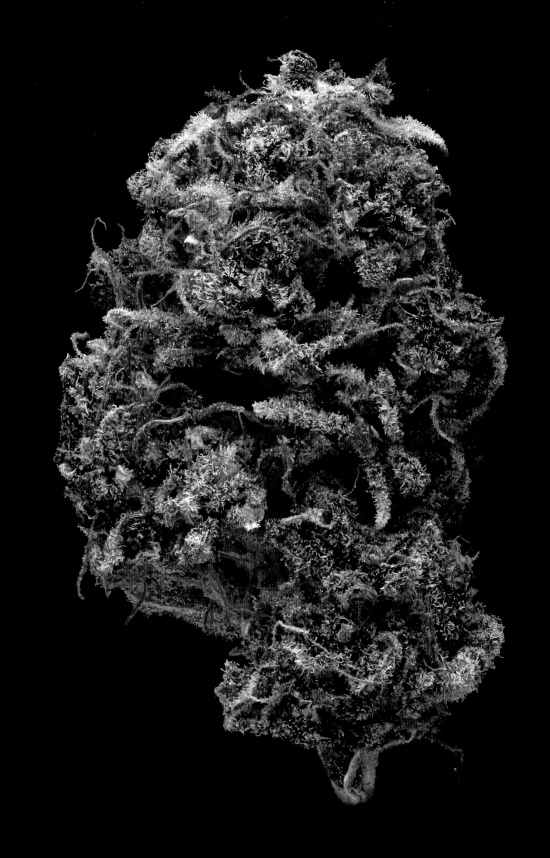

STRAIN NAME
Purple OG ●

TYPE
indica hybrid ●

LINEAGE
OG Kush × (Urkel × Trainwreck)

SMELL/TASTE
grape, sweet, fuel

COMMON EFFECTS
euphoria, relaxed, sleepy

TOP MEDICINAL USES
appetite, insomnia

SIMILAR STRAINS
Mr. Nice Guy ● p/264
GDP ● p/178
God's Gift ● p/186

———————

Purple OG has the looks, the flavors, and the effects that make it a well-rounded bud. The flower's violet coloring is wildly saturated and distinct. The aromas bring out a nose-tingling grape fuel that tastes exactly as it smells. And just one hit of Purple OG is all you'll need to feel the effects of this extremely potent flower. The euphoric sedation reaches every body part and intensifies with no end, so it's best to enjoy Purple OG before bedtime.

STRAIN NAME

Purple Sticky Punch●

TYPE
indica ●

LINEAGE
Afghani × Purple AK-47

SMELL/TASTE
earthy, creamy, musky

COMMON EFFECTS
sleepy, body buzz, relaxed

TOP MEDICINAL USES
insomnia, anxiety

SIMILAR STRAINS
GDP ● p/178
Lavender ● p/244
Blueberry Yum Yum ● p/108

Purple Sticky Punch's flowers have a unique wild, rough, and "outdoorsy" look to them. The clumpy bud breaks up nicely into a sticky pile of dense little nuggets. The aromas and flavors are very earthy with a creamy smoke that is quite smooth and enjoyable. Purple Sticky packs a physical punch that instantly wipes out all energy and drops you down into a couch-locking slumber.

STRAIN NAME

Querkle ●

TYPE
indica hybrid ●

LINEAGE
Urkle × Space Queen

SMELL/TASTE
grape, fruity, musty

COMMON EFFECTS
euphoria, relaxed, mellow

TOP MEDICINAL USES
stress, anxiety

SIMILAR STRAINS
Purple Sticky Punch ● p/312
Burkle ● p/116
Mr. Nice Guy ● p/264

Querkle is an interesting hybrid that has two distinct phenotypes. One is a shorter, purple indica bomb, while the other (shown here) is more reminiscent of its Space Queen parent with a more balanced hybrid high. The smells and flavors are a sharp grape mixed with a dank fruity twist, making for a big-hitting clean smoke. The effect is a mellow, stoney high that's long lasting and not exhausting.

STRAIN NAME

Red Congo

TYPE
sativa ●

LINEAGE
Congolese Sativa × (Mexican ×
Afghani)

SMELL/TASTE
sweet, pungent, citrus

COMMON EFFECTS
focused, alert, creative

TOP MEDICINAL USES
mood enhancement, anxiety

AWARDS
Medical Cannabis Cup

SIMILAR STRAINS
Congolese Sativa ● p/150
Chernobyl ● p/134
Chocolope ● p/144

Three powerful landraces join forces to
create a slow-burning sativa famous for its
clearheaded effects. From its long, fluffy
buds and crisp clean aromas to its airy
smoke and easy high, everything about
Red Congo is lighthearted. A subtle head-
to-toe tingle is accompanied by a clear,
sharp focus that amplifies all your senses
and provides optimistic motivation
throughout your high.

STRAIN NAME
Rock Star●

TYPE
indica hybrid ●

LINEAGE
Rock Bud × Sensi Star

SMELL/TASTE
spicy, earthy, fruity

COMMON EFFECTS
relaxed, mellow, cheerful

TOP MEDICINAL USES
muscle tension, appetite

AWARDS
Cannabis Cup

SIMILAR STRAINS
Afghani ● p/56
Dead Head OG ● p/160
Northern Lights #5 ● p/270

These deep-colored nugs are as plump and tightly packed as they come and offer a full-bodied smoke that is just as dense. Rock Star's aromas and flavors are not overpowering but have a nice pungent earthiness that's very cinnamon in its taste. The effect is a clearheaded stone that is not as heavy as you might expect from an indica-dominant hybrid, but the full-body tingle makes for a long-lasting mellow and functioning stone.

STRAIN NAME

Romulan ●

TYPE
indica hybrid ●

LINEAGE
unknown (British Columbia)

SMELL/TASTE
peppery, berry, woody

COMMON EFFECTS
mellow, lazy, cheerful

TOP MEDICINAL USES
pain, stress

SIMILAR STRAINS
Blackberry Kush ● p/88
Hash Plant ● p/200
Sugar Daddy ● p/354

This Canadian legend has a fabled history fit for its science fiction name, believed to have Colombian, Mexican, Afghani, and even Korean genetics. With an unknown origin, it's almost believable that this hybrid actually comes from the *Star Trek* planet of Romulus—especially after you've smoked some of this mysterious bud. Believed to be mostly indica, thanks to its narcotic body buzz, Romulan will surprise you with its mind-altering abilities. Your head and body will feel like what a Romulus alien's forehead looks like— totally dented.

STRAIN NAME

Romulan Berry ●

TYPE
indica hybrid ●

LINEAGE
Romulan × Blueberry

SMELL/TASTE
pungent, fruity, berry

COMMON EFFECTS
cheerful, mellow, euphoria

TOP MEDICINAL USES
anxiety, appetite

SIMILAR STRAINS
Goo Berry ● p/188
Sour Grape ● p/346
Grape Ape ● p/190

Romulan Berry, sometimes referred to simply as Romberry, adds the pleasant taste of Blueberry to the balanced indica effects of the mysterious Romulan strain. The flavors are sweet and fruity with a smoke that's wispy smooth and light, allowing for nice big flavorful tokes. The effects are very similar to Romulan with a more mellow body high and a happy mental buzz that keeps away any tiredness or laziness.

STRAIN NAME

SFV OG ●

TYPE
hybrid ●

LINEAGE
OG Kush phenotype

SMELL/TASTE
acrid, fuel, piney

COMMON EFFECTS
euphoria, cheerful, focused

TOP MEDICINAL USES
stress, mood enhancement

AWARDS
Cannabis Cup, Medical Cannabis Cup

SIMILAR STRAINS
Ghost ● p/180
Holy Grail ● p/214
XXX OG ● p/390

SFV OG (for San Fernando Valley in California) is an elite OG Kush cut. SFV's strong lemon cleaner aromas will fill the room, while the fuel-filled pine flavor fills your palate with this well-known kush taste. The smoke is thick and expansive, bringing on effects that are the best of both worlds—a rush of cerebral bliss with an invigorating body buzz that leaves your entire system relaxed and calm.

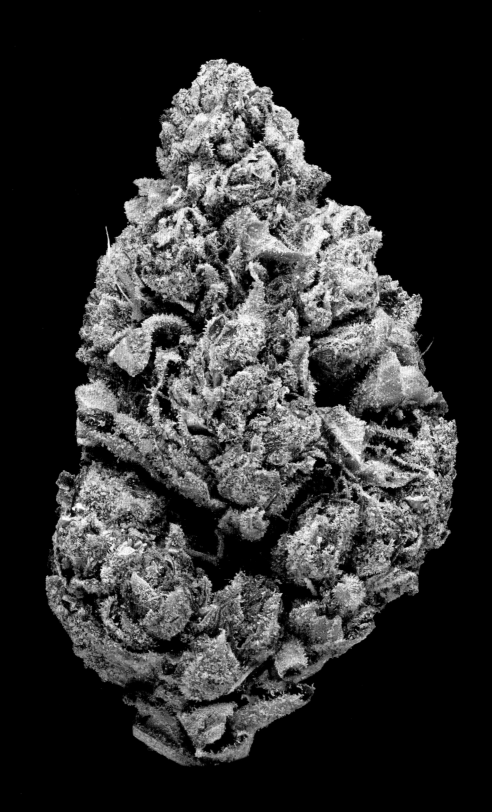

STRAIN NAME

Shire

TYPE
sativa

LINEAGE
Super Silver Haze × Sour Diesel

SMELL/TASTE
pungent, fuel, lemon

COMMON EFFECTS
cheerful, uplifted, psychedelic

TOP MEDICINAL USES
mood enhancement, stress

SIMILAR STRAINS
Super Lemon Haze p/358
Lemon Skunk p/246
Snocap p/332

Shire is a supercross of two very potent sativas. Its pungent aromas cannot be contained, with its jet-fueled lemon smells escaping anything you try to store these dense nugs into. The flavor and smoke are just as strong as its aroma and are clear indicators of the sheer strength of this sativa. The strong cerebral effects are extremely overpowering and take over the mind with a focused energy that wakes up the imagination.

STRAIN NAME
Skunk #1 ●

TYPE
hybrid ●

LINEAGE
Afghani × Mexican × Colombian

SMELL/TASTE
skunky, pungent, acrid

COMMON EFFECTS
uplifting, body buzz, euphoria

TOP MEDICINAL USES
stress, anxiety

AWARDS
Cannabis Cup
Spannabis Cup

SIMILAR STRAINS
Cheese ● p/128
Haze ● p/204
Chemdawg ● p/132

Developed in the late 1970s, Skunk #1 is one of the most important hybrids ever bred. By fusing together a lineage of genetic all-stars, Skunk #1 produces a fast-acting and soaring high that is balanced by an uplifting full-body buzz—resulting in a model hybrid high. And its ubiquitous skunky aroma and flavor has now become synonymous with high-quality chronic. Skunk #1 is living proof of the value of experimenting and crossbreeding plants and is now used as a building block in some of the most popular hybrids being developed and grown today.

STRAIN NAME

Skywalker ●

TYPE
indica ●

LINEAGE
Mazar × Blueberry

SMELL/TASTE
skunk, piney, musty, lemon

COMMON EFFECTS
sleepy, couch-lock, lazy

TOP MEDICINAL USES
insomnia, pain

SIMILAR STRAINS
True OG ● p/376
Louis XIII ● p/248
Tahoe OG ● p/368

Skywalker *is* the Jedi knight of couch-lock strains. It provides a body-melting therapeutic high that is fast acting and long lasting. You will feel your eyes begin to close as soon as you pop these dense nugs out of their jar. Even though the aroma and visual appeal are pretty standard, this strain's natural sleep aid benefit is what makes it a world-renowned medicine.

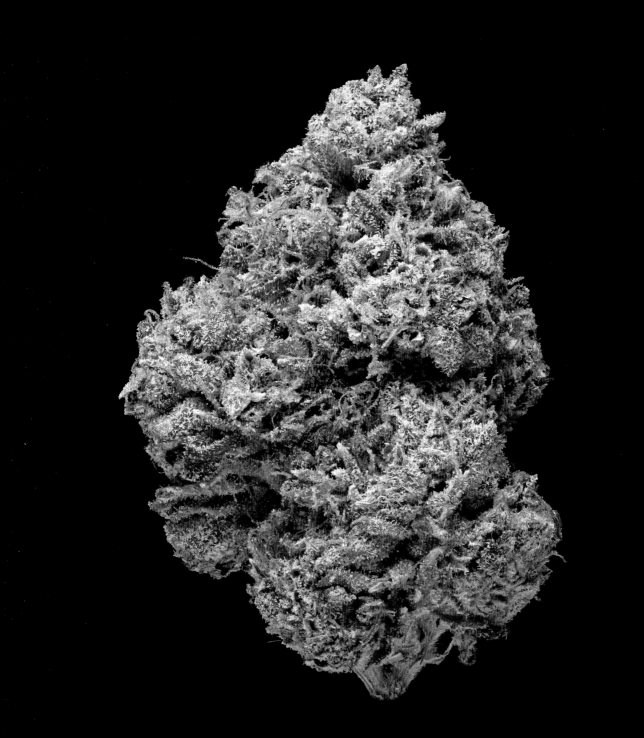

STRAIN NAME
Snocap

TYPE
sativa hybrid ●

LINEAGE
Humboldt Snow × Unknown Haze

SMELL/TASTE
lemon, minty, astringent

COMMON EFFECTS
uplifted, euphoria, focused

TOP MEDICINAL USES
mood enhancement, stress

SIMILAR STRAINS
Shire ● p/326
Lemon Skunk ● p/246
Jack Herer ● p/222

Snocap is a relaxing sativa hybrid with an undeniable Haze lineage. This sticky flower has a powerful lemon-citrus acrid smell that intensifies as you break the squishy bud apart. A nice minty aftertaste completes a smooth smoke that hits big and fast. Snocap's hazy potency kicks in with a spacey head rush that quickly evens out into a very clear, high-functioning, and motivating high.

STRAIN NAME

Sour Amnesia ●

TYPE
sativa hybrid ●

LINEAGE
Amnesia × Sour Diesel

SMELL/TASTE
spicy, fuel, skunky

COMMON EFFECTS
energetic, uplifting, cheerful

TOP MEDICINAL USES
fatigue, mood enhancement

AWARDS
Cannabis Cup

SIMILAR STRAINS
Sour Chelumbian ● p/338
Sour LA ● p/348
Sour Dawg ● p/340

Amsterdam's finest meets New York's best to produce this very powerful supersativa hybrid. The flowers are big, fat, and completely covered in thick trichome crystals. Sour Amnesia's skunky, jet-fueled flavor hits big and deep—expanding your lungs and immediately expanding your mind with a soaring and stimulating sativa high.

STRAIN NAME

Sour Bubble ●

TYPE
hybrid ●

LINEAGE
Sour Diesel × Bubble Gum

SMELL/TASTE
sweet, citrus, fuel

COMMON EFFECTS
uplifting, alert, relaxing

TOP MEDICINAL USES
stress, nausea

SIMILAR STRAINS
Sour Dubble ● p/344
Ogiesel ● p/280
Cannalope Haze ● p/120

The pure indica Bubble Gum genetics are a nice companion to the overpowering Sour Diesel traits that create this well-balanced hybrid. The aromas are definitely fuel filled, while the flavors are on the sweet side with an overall sour bubble gum taste. Sour Bubble produces a clearheaded motivational push followed by a gentle body relaxation to round out the perfectly hybrid high.

STRAIN NAME

Sour Chelumbian

TYPE
sativa hybrid ●

LINEAGE
Sour Diesel × (UK Cheese × Columbian Gold)

SMELL/TASTE
spicy, fuel, berry

COMMON EFFECTS
creative, cheerful, focused

TOP MEDICINAL USES
mood enhancement, anxiety

SIMILAR STRAINS
Sour Diesel ● p/342
Sour Dawg ● p/340
Pure Gold ● p/304

This intricate hybrid mix takes the distinct characteristics from its long line of genetics and combines them into one supersativa hybrid. Cheese, diesel, skunk, berry, and a unique crisp celery flavor are all intertwined into a very complex and rich flavor profile. The sativa high will put all your senses on high alert with a light energy and mellow body buzz, making Sour Chelumbian a wonderful wake and bake strain.

STRAIN NAME

Sour Dawg

TYPE
sativa hybrid ●

LINEAGE
Sour Diesel × Chemdawg

SMELL/TASTE
tart, fuel, lemon

COMMON EFFECTS
cheerful, uplifted, euphoria

TOP MEDICINAL USES
stress, nausea

SIMILAR STRAINS
Sour Amnesia ● p/334
Crystal Coma ● p/156
Sour LA ● p/348

Sour Dawg is like a rabid version of Sour Diesel, but much more potent, and much more aggressive. This gnarly nug has a jet-fueled bite that'll make you pucker with every puff of its intoxicating smoke. This cerebral blast hits fast and blankets the mind and body in an escalating euphoria and deep elation. This sativa high can be overpowering and racy, making Sour Dawg a one and done toke.

STRAIN NAME

Sour Diesel ●

TYPE
sativa hybrid ●

LINEAGE
Chemdawg × Mass Superskunk

SMELL/TASTE
fuel, citrus, tart

COMMON EFFECTS
euphoria, energetic, alert

TOP MEDICINAL USES
stress, anxiety

AWARD
Cannabis Cup

SIMILAR STRAINS
Larry OG ● p/242
Crystal Coma ● p/156
Sour LA ● p/348

Sour Diesel is arguably one of the most extreme and famous sativa strains in the world. Its distinct and intoxicating aroma will fill up a room with scents of lemon and diesel gas (in a good way) and its fast-acting psychedelic high will shoot straight to your brain and fill you up with copious amounts of good uplifting energy. "Sour D" made a name for itself on the East Coast and is still one of the most widely smoked and sought-after strains of all time—this bud truly is the Diesel of all dank.

STRAIN NAME

Sour Dubble

TYPE
hybrid ●

LINEAGE
Sour Diesel × Sour Bubble

SMELL/TASTE
sweet, fuel, fruity

COMMON EFFECTS
uplifting, relaxing, cheerful

TOP MEDICINAL USES
appetite, anxiety

SIMILAR STRAINS
Sour Bubble ● p/336
Sour LA ● p/348
Platinum Bubba ● p/296

This dank little nugget is a pungent power flower. Sour Dubble emits a very strong double-diesel fuel aroma with a flavor that's noticeably sweet and fruity. The instant head buzz is fast and stimulating but gets paired down with a relaxing body stone that's light and calming. Overall, the high is an uplifting experience without any heavy stone sedation.

STRAIN NAME

Sour Grape ●

TYPE
hybrid ●

LINEAGE
Grape Ape × Sour Diesel

SMELL/TASTE
grape, lemon, fuel

COMMON EFFECTS
uplifted, cheerful, body buzz

TOP MEDICINAL USES
nausea, anxiety

AWARD
Medical Cannabis Cup

SIMILAR STRAINS
GDP ● p/178
Cotton Candy ● p/152
Purple OG ● p/310

The appealing pastel purples and frosty oranges give Sour Grape an alluring bag appeal. The good looks are perfectly complemented by the complex sour-grape sweetness of the aromas. The flavorful smoke is expansive and thick, hitting hard and fast. Sour Grape's effects are a true hybrid of its parents, a balanced mix of energy and calm that soothe the body and boost the mind.

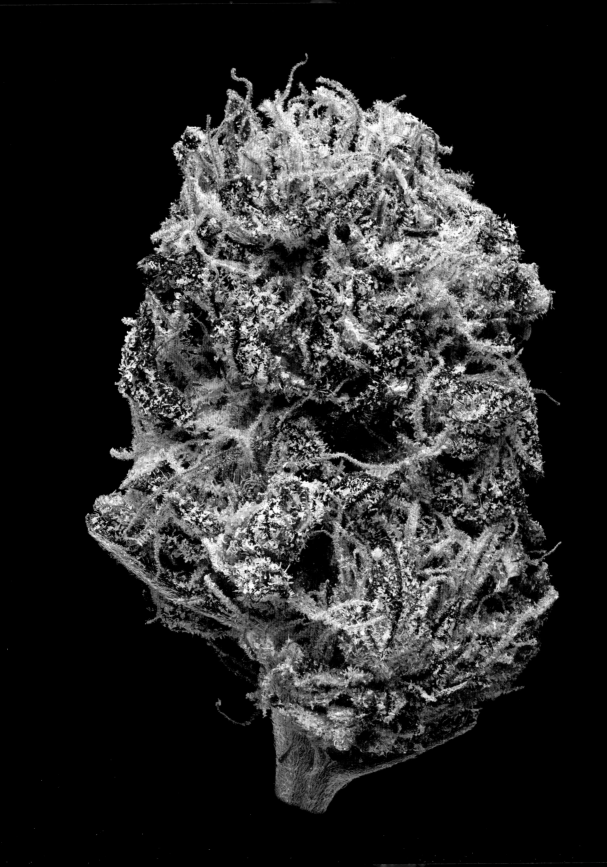

STRAIN NAME

Sour LA ●

TYPE
hybrid ●

LINEAGE
Sour Diesel × LA Confidential

SMELL/TASTE
lemon, piney, skunky

COMMON EFFECTS
euphoria, cheerful, body buzz

TOP MEDICINAL USES
stress, anxiety

SIMILAR STRAINS
Sour Dubble ● p/344
Crystal Coma ● p/156
Pink Pearl ● p/294

Sour LA joins the legendary East Coast sativa with the famous West Coast indica to create a hybrid that's a perfect balance of these polar-opposite strains. The pungent aroma is tart and compounds the sweet, skunky flavors. The smoke hits heavy and hard to fully expand the lungs with its fuel-filled power. The effects are fast acting, uplifting to the mind and body with a rush of energy that tickles your entire system. The powerful hybrid high eliminates any of the couch-lock its LA Confidential side is prone to produce, leaving the body relaxed but not stoney.

STRAIN NAME
Space Queen ●

TYPE
hybrid ●

LINEAGE
Romulan × Cinderella 99

SMELL/TASTE
fruity, floral, sweet

COMMON EFFECTS
focused, uplifting, creative

TOP MEDICINAL USES
stress, nausea

SIMILAR STRAINS
Jack Herer ● p/222
Afgoo ● p/58
Lemon Skunk ● p/246

Space Queen is an interesting cross of two intriguing parents. The end result is a haze-like high that immediately lifts off to a clear head-space. The high finishes off nicely with a slow descent that travels through the rest of your body—mellowing out the spacey high for a soft landing. Space Queen's strong genetics has made this strain a reliable building block when creating other modern hybrids.

STRAIN NAME

Strawberry Cough ●

TYPE
sativa hybrid ●

LINEAGE
Haze × Strawberry Fields

SMELL/TASTE
strawberry, cedar, earthy

COMMON EFFECTS
sociable, cheerful, focused

TOP MEDICINAL USES
fatigue, mood enhancement

AWARD
Cannabis Cup

SIMILAR STRAINS
Tangie ● p/370
Afgoo ● p/58
Dirty Hairy ● p/164

These one-of-a-kind buds are a delicious variety worthy of its sought-after name. Originally hailing from the tiny state of Connecticut, Strawberry Cough has received worldwide fame for its rich, flavorful smoke and soaring high. The flavor and aroma are a complex mix of creamy strawberry and a hazy cedar wood that fill the air with sweet incense. The uplifting high is clearly sativa dominant and elicits a positive and focused sensation that seems to put all your senses on high alert.

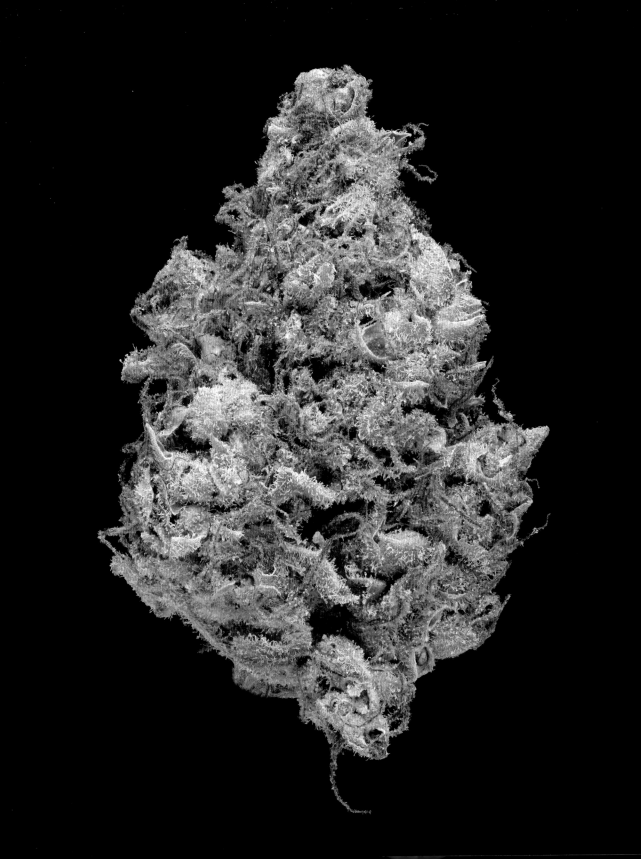

STRAIN NAME

Sugar Daddy ●

TYPE
indica ●

LINEAGE
California Indica × Sugar Blossoms

SMELL/TASTE
peppery, lemon, earthy

COMMON EFFECTS
relaxed, mellow, lazy

TOP MEDICINAL USES
stress, nausea

SIMILAR STRAINS
Sugar Shack ● p/356
Romulan Berry ● p/322
Blackberry Kush ● p/88

Sugar Daddy's name comes from its looks not its flavors. These wildly leafy buds have an amazing structure and coloring that is out-shined by the tremendous amount of sugary crystals that shoot from all over like gooey goose bumps. This plant is very much an indica and has an old-school kushy smell and flavor profile. The traditional stoney kick will provide a long-lasting body relaxation.

STRAIN NAME

Sugar Shack ●

TYPE
indica hybrid ●

LINEAGE
unknown (Canada)

SMELL/TASTE
sweet, piney, peppery

COMMON EFFECTS
sleepy, Euphoria, couch-lock

TOP MEDICINAL USES
appetite, insomnia

SIMILAR STRAINS
Sugar Daddy ● p/354
Platinum Bubba ● p/296
Ingrid ● p/216

Sugar Shack is an archetypal indica hybrid. The dense, leafy nugs have a deep green coloring and dark orange hairs that appear to stand up with a sugar coating of trichomes. The aromas and flavors are a contrasting mix of sweet and spicy with an overall pinesap fragrance. The smoke is thick and expansive, producing a jaded stone that creeps and mellows out into a sleepy retreat.

STRAIN NAME

Super Lemon Haze ●

TYPE
sativa hybrid ●

LINEAGE
Super Silver Haze × Lemon Skunk

SMELL/TASTE
sour, citrus, menthol, fruity

COMMON EFFECTS
uplifting, energetic, creative

TOP MEDICINAL USES
anxiety, mood enhancement

AWARDS
Cannabis Cup, Medical Cannabis Cup, Spannabis Cup

SIMILAR STRAINS
Trainwreck ● p/372
Green Ribbon ● p/196
Lemon Skunk ● p/246

Creating this hybrid involved a mad-scientist approach by first crossing two coveted strains, Skunk #1 and Northern Lights, each with a unique Haze hybrid. Those two strains were then combined into one perfect sativa-dominate superhero. Its superpowered high races through your head, giving an uncanny energy that is sharp and progressive. Supergenetics, superdank, superhazy—Super Lemon Haze *is* a supersativa.

STRAIN NAME

Super Silver Haze ●

TYPE
sativa hybrid ●

LINEAGE
(Skunk #1 × [Haze × Haze]) ×
(Northern Lights #5 × [Haze × Haze])

SMELL/TASTE
earthy, sweet, spicy

COMMON EFFECTS
body buzz, euphoria, uplifted

TOP MEDICINAL USES
Mood Enhancement, Nausea

AWARDS
Cannabis Cup, Highlife Cup

SIMILAR STRAINS
White Widow ● p/386
Amnesia Haze ● p/70
Shire ● p/326

Another perfect example of an Amsterdam Haze, Super Silver Haze combines the finest characteristics of Skunk, Northern Lights, and Haze into one great Dutch ganja. The flavors are a pleasant mix of sweet and spicy with a smoke that is as hazy as they come. The stone is a full head-to-toe experience that produces a long-lasting and energetic body high that is never a disappointment.

STRAIN NAME

Super Silver Pearl

TYPE
sativa hybrid

LINEAGE
Silver Pearl × Super Silver Haze

SMELL/TASTE
spicy, sweet, creamy

COMMON EFFECTS
psychedelic, energetic, euphoria

TOP MEDICINAL USES
fatigue, mood enhancement

SIMILAR STRAINS
Super Lemon Haze p/358
Vanilla Haze p/380
White Widow p/386

Simply put, Super Silver Pearl is some extreme chronic. The tall bud structure has a crisp green coloring with plenty of bright orange hairs to attract the long, sticky trichomes that cover the entire flower. The aromas have a sweet creaminess that translates into a more spicy and almost dark chocolate-like flavor. The smoke packs a superpunch and should be treated as a one-hit wonder with mental effects that will have your head soaring without slowing down.

STRAIN NAME

Super Skunk ●

TYPE
hybrid ●

LINEAGE
Skunk #1 × Afghani

SMELL/TASTE
skunk, citrus, pepper, spicy

COMMON EFFECTS
happy, spacey, lazy

TOP MEDICINAL USES
stress, pain

AWARDS
Cannabis Cup, Highlife Cup

SIMILAR STRAINS
Hash Plant ● p/200
P91 ● p/286
Trainwreck ● p/372

This superstrain was specifically cultivated for serious lovers of skunk cheebas. Super Skunk's claim to fame is the overwhelming stench of its dank skunk-like odor (in a good way, of course) commonly associated with good skunk strains. The Afghani influences are apparent in the relaxed state you will enter, while the Skunk ancestry will produce a nicely balanced ratio of body-to-head effects. Super Skunk can produce a strong couch-lock if you overindulge, making this strain better for an evening-to-nighttime session.

STRAIN NAME

Sweet Tooth ●

TYPE
indica hybrid ●

LINEAGE
Grapefruit × (Sweet Pink Grapefruit × Blueberry)

SMELL/TASTE
citrus, berry, bubble gum

COMMON EFFECTS
uplifting, body buzz, relaxed

TOP MEDICINAL USES
pain, appetite

AWARD
Cannabis Cup

SIMILAR STRAINS
Juicy Fruit ● p/230
Dirty Hairy ● p/164
Grape Romulan ● p/192

Sweet Tooth's sugary crystals and supertight buds produce a complex mix of flavors and effects. Fresh citrus, tart berry, and fruity bubble gum make for a distinct smoke flavor that expands the lungs with thick, creamy smoke. The indica-dominant effects are perfectly balanced with an uplifting cerebral high that fights off the sleepiness of the super-strong body stone, creating a sweet, stoney high.

STRAIN NAME

Tahoe OG ●

TYPE
hybrid ●

LINEAGE
Tahoe Kush × SFV OG

SMELL/TASTE
piney, spicy, earthy

COMMON EFFECTS
sleepy, couch-lock, lazy

TOP MEDICINAL USES
insomnia, appetite, pain

AWARD
Cannabis Cup

SIMILAR STRAINS
True OG ● p/376
XXX OG ● p/390
Godfather OG ● p/184

This potent Kush hybrid is a popular medical strain and a sleeper, as in it will literally put you to sleep. This is one of the strongest medical testing strains available with THC levels consistently surpassing 25%. This particular OG is heavy on the indica side and is prone to couch-locks and zone outs, so it's best to save this strain for a rainy day or a late-night session. The smoke is smooth and filling and a puff or two will do just fine.

STRAIN NAME

Tangie ●

TYPE
sativa hybrid ●

LINEAGE
Tangerine × Super Silver Haze

SMELL/TASTE
citrus, tangerine, sweet

COMMON EFFECTS
uplifted, creative, cheerful

TOP MEDICINAL USES
stress, nausea

AWARDS
Cannabis Cup, Medical Cannabis Cup

SIMILAR STRAINS
Cherry AK ● p/136
Durban Poison ● p/166
Pineapple Express ● p/292

The clear and refreshing tangerine aroma is what makes Tangie such a special hybrid. The resin-soaked buds complement the intense aromas nicely and breaking up this flower is a sticky and stinky delight. The flavors are strong on the citrus tastes with a pleasant skunky overtone on the exhale. Tangie stimulates the mind with its clear sativa influence, making it a nice strain for daytime activities and socializing.

STRAIN NAME

Trainwreck ●

TYPE
hybrid ●

LINEAGE
Mexican × Thai × Afghani

SMELL/TASTE
peppery, citrus, fuel

COMMON EFFECTS
euphoria, energetic, body buzz

TOP MEDICINAL USES
stress, pain

SIMILAR STRAINS
Jack Herer ● p/222
Super Lemon Haze ● p/358
White Widow ● p/386

Developed out of Humboldt County in the late 1980s, Trainwreck is one of the strongest hybrids to come out of California and is highly sought after by medical marijuana users for its well-rounded therapeutic qualities. Smoking Trainwreck is a total rush that hits hard and fast just like the name suggests. It produces a euphoric, heady high coupled with a nice body buzz that will send your mind soaring and relax you just enough to remain grounded. Its unique genetics also make this strain a popular breeding plant found in many other hybrids.

STRAIN NAME

Triangle ●

TYPE
hybrid ●

LINEAGE
OG Kush phenotype

SMELL/TASTE
piney, lemon, spicy

COMMON EFFECTS
alert, sociable, creative

TOP MEDICINAL USES
stress, anxiety

SIMILAR STRAINS
Ghost ● p/180
OG Kush ● p/278
SFV OG ● p/324

Triangle is a rare OG Kush strain that hails from Florida and believed by many insiders to be the mother of all the OG Kush varieties. Triangle is named after the line that connects the threes cities of Florida known for their marijuana cultivation—Jacksonville, Miami, and Tampa. From its old-school appearance, pungent flavor, and stimulating effects, Triangle is a superhero version of OG Kush with all the world-class characteristics amplified, fine-tuned, and at peak performance.

STRAIN NAME

True OG ●

TYPE
indica ●

LINEAGE
unknown (California)

SMELL/TASTE
piney, earthy, minty

COMMON EFFECTS
body buzz, couch-lock, euphoric

TOP MEDICINAL USES
pain, muscle tension

SIMILAR STRAINS
Abusive OG ● p/54
Tahoe OG ● p/368
XXX OG ● p/390

—————

True OG is a hard-hitting indica strain with intense kush-like scents and flavors. The buds are solid and bulky with vibrant colors that are as extraordinary as their pungent aromas. The playfully thick smoke is ultrasmooth and hits very fast. This Southern California flower offers "true" indica effects that are long lasting and heavy-eyed. The stoney high begins with a pulsating euphoria and transitions into a full-body relaxation—ending in a deep and tranquil repose.

STRAIN NAME

Ultra Blue Romulan ●

TYPE
hybrid ●

LINEAGE
Blue Cheese × Romulan

SMELL/TASTE
fruity, skunky, musky

COMMON EFFECTS
euphoria, focused, mellow

TOP MEDICINAL USES
appetite, mood enhancement

SIMILAR STRAINS
Washington ● p/384
Chernobyl ● p/134
Jack the Ripper ● p/224

Ultra Blue Romulan is a strain with definite bag appeal. The perfectly squishy and dense nugs have the ideal combination of contrasting greens and oranges, and the trichome crystal covering goes deep and shimmers with a crystal-blue light. The aromas are pungent and skunky, while the smoke flavor is reminiscent of a blueberry muffin. The effects are a hybrid mix that results in a mild high that's both mellow and engaging.

STRAIN NAME
Vanilla Haze ●

TYPE
hybrid ●

LINEAGE
Blueberry × Super Silver Haze

SMELL/TASTE
spicy, vanilla, fruity

COMMON EFFECTS
uplifted, relaxed, cheerful

TOP MEDICINAL USES
appetite, stress

SIMILAR STRAINS
Super Lemon Haze ● p/358
White Widow ● p/386
Super Silver Pearl ● p/362

————

This exotic-tasting, sativa-dominant hybrid grows in long, wispy buds, but don't let its thin, lanky appearance fool you. This is a very potent strain with an uplifting and insanely strong and long-lasting high. The high level of haze potency makes it a great choice for a "wake 'n' bake" or for daytime use. Unfortunately, growers are not too eager to produce this strain because of the small yields the plant produces, making this strain difficult to come by.

STRAIN NAME

Velvet Haze

TYPE
sativa hybrid ●

LINEAGE
Blue Velvet × Haze

SMELL/TASTE
earthy, skunky, musky

COMMON EFFECTS
uplifted, alert, body buzz

TOP MEDICINAL USES
anxiety, pain

SIMILAR STRAINS
Blueberry Afgoo ● p/106
Grape Ape ● p/190
Berry White ● p/74

These golden buds shine with an expansive coating of amber crystals that cover every surface of Velvet Haze's tall and compacted structure. The aroma is very earthy with a taste that's a hazy mix of skunk and spice flavors that hit quick and smooth. A visually stunning sativa specimen, Velvet Haze offers a nice combination of mental and body effects that make for a stoney, functioning high.

STRAIN NAME

Washington

TYPE
sativa hybrid ●

LINEAGE
Jack Herer × OG Kush

SMELL/TASTE
floral, fruity, minty

COMMON EFFECTS
sociable, cheerful, uplifted

TOP MEDICINAL USES
stress, mood elevation

SIMILAR STRAINS
Ultra Blue Romulan ● p/378
Jack the Ripper ● p/224
XJ-13 ● p/388

Named after the original President George Washington, this chronic perfectly honors his infamous stature. The appearance of Washington is enough to seduce the senses with its forest-green coloring and squishy, dense structure that is wrapped with groomed hairs and covered in sparkling trichomes. The flavors and aromas are evocative of its forefathers, Jack Herer and OG Kush, and it effect is a sweeping rush of head-to-toe euphoria.

STRAIN NAME

White Widow ●

TYPE
hybrid ●

LINEAGE
Indian indica × Brazilian sativa

SMELL/TASTE
pungent, earthy, peppery

COMMON EFFECTS
focused, euphoria, body buzz

TOP MEDICINAL USES
stress, anxiety

AWARDS
Cannabis Cup, Highlife Cup

SIMILAR STRAINS
Congolese Sativa ● p/150
Cherry Pie ● p/138
Super Silver Haze ● p/360

White Widow is a visual juggernaut. The buds are perfectly dense and compact and the crystals that rest on the light green buds seem to coat every single part of this luscious flower. White Widow is so frosty it looks as if its been dipped in pure white sugar. This famed strain has been mentioned by name in songs and television shows and has spawned a full family of other famed White strains. You can expect an uplifting and thought provoking high accompanied by a perfect full-bodied buzz. White Widow is a fun, functional, and sociable stone.

STRAIN NAME

XJ-13 ●

TYPE
hybrid ●

LINEAGE
G-13 × Jack Herer

SMELL/TASTE
lime, piney, spicy

COMMON EFFECTS
uplifting, focused, alert

TOP MEDICINAL USES
nausea, anxiety

SIMILAR STRAINS
J1 ● p/220
Jack the Ripper ● p/224
Jack Skellington ● p/226

XJ-13 is a sativa-dominant hybrid that is the product of two very potent and popular strains: G-13 and Jack Herer. The XJ-13 plant is known for its large cola buds and has a very low leaf-to-bud ratio. Its buds are neon green in color and are covered in pristine trichomes. The hybrid effects can be felt instantly—starting with a fun and energizing rush and transitioning into a nice relaxing body buzz.

STRAIN NAME

XXX OG ●

TYPE
hybrid ●

LINEAGE
OG Kush phenotype

SMELL/TASTE
piney, earthy, minty

COMMON EFFECTS
body buzz, alert, euphoria

TOP MEDICINAL USES
pain, muscle tension

AWARD
Medical Cannabis Cup

SIMILAR STRAINS
Abusive OG ● p/54
Tahoe OG ● p/368
True OG ● p/376

XXX OG, a.k.a. Triple OG, is yet another variety of the famed OG Kush. Visually, XXX OG is a brighter and more voluminous bud than its sister strains. Aside from its looks, everything else screams OG, from the trademark kushy flavors to the blissful body buzz and clear head. The flavors and effects XXX OG produces can be a bit more overwhelming and heavy than the rest of the family, so a few gentle tokes will do just fine.

BUDS BY STRAIN TYPE

sativa

sativa hybrid

hybrid

sativa	sativa hybrid			hybrid		
	Old Mendo Haze	Cherry Pie Kush	Lucid Dream	Super Silver Haze	Blue Diesel	Dirty Hairy
	Panama Red	Chocolate Thunder	Motorbreath	Super Silver Pearl	Blue Dream	Dutch Treat
	Red Congo	Chocolope	NYC Diesel	Tangie	Blue Nightmare	Fire OG
Allen Wrench	Shire	Chiesel	P91	Velvet Haze	Blueberry Yum Yum	Fruity Pebbles
Cannalope Haze	Afwreck	Cinderella 99	Pineapple	Washington	Bubble Gum	Ghost
Congolese Sativa	Alpha Blue	Euphoria	Pineapple Express	5Gs x OGSD	Cannatonic	Girl Scout Cookies
Durban Poison	Amnesia Haze	Green Crack	Snocap	Abusive OG	Champagne	Grape Romulan
Hawaiian Sativa	Blue Hawaiian	Harlequin	Sour Amnesia	Agent Orange	Cheese (U.K. Cheese)	Green Ribbon
Haze	Candy Chem	Head Cheese	Sour Chelumbian	AK-47	Cherry Pie	Headband
Jack Herer	Chemband	Island Sweet Skunk	Sour Dawg	Berry White	Crystal Coma	Hempstar
King's Bread	Chemdawg	J1	Sour Diesel	Bio Diesel	Daywrecker	Holy Grail
Lamb's Bread	Chernobyl	Jack the Ripper	Strawberry Cough	Black Cherry Soda	Dead Head OG	Jack Skellington
Maui Waui	Cherry AK	Lemon Skunk	Super Lemon Haze	Blackberry	Death Star	Jillybean